Watching

TOM SUTCLIFFE

faber and faber

LONDON · NEW YORK

First published in 2000
by Faber and Faber Limited
3 Queen Square London WC1N 3AU
Published in the United States by Faber and Faber Inc.
a division of Farrar, Straus and Giroux Inc., New York

Phototypeset by Intype London Ltd
Printed in England by Clays Ltd, St Ives plc

Tom Sutcliffe is hereby identified as author of this
work in accordance with Section 77 of the Copyright,
Designs and Patents Act 1988

A CIP record for this book
is available from the British Library

ISBN 0-571-19036-7 ✓

2 4 6 8 10 9 7 5 3 1

To Deborah

CONTENTS

Projection

1/ a. The casting of some ingredient into a crucible: esp. in Alchemy, the casting of the powder of philosopher's stone (powder of projection) upon a metal in fusion to effect its transmutation into gold or silver.

2/ a. The action of projecting, or fact of being optically projected, as a figure or image, against a background. The process of projecting an image on a film or transparency on to a screen for viewing.

3/ Psychoanal. The unconscious process or fact of projecting one's fears, feelings, desires or fantasies on to other persons, things or situations.

OXFORD ENGLISH DICTIONARY

'Why is it that we can't tell a lie through a flashback?' Alfred Hitchcock once mused, in the course of a long and reverential interview conducted by François Truffaut. What Hitchcock had in mind was the section in his own film *Stage Fright* in which the audience are offered a misleading flashback, a sequence that later turns out not to have represented a real state of affairs at all. It's clear that he didn't have a *technical* impossibility in mind here – after all, it's extremely easy to tell a lie in flashback, in part because the audience is so trusting. Hitchcock had achieved it and other directors have done it since. Indeed, *The Usual Suspects*, Bryan Singer's narrative cadenza about a mysterious criminal mastermind, could be said to be almost nothing but a flashback that tells a lie. But *The Usual Suspects* is conspicuously a film about the way in which storytelling is a collaborative venture between the plausibility of the storyteller and the desire of the listener for coherence, so it is able to recover from the audacious moment at which it finally comes clean. Even so, it divided audiences between those who were delighted to have been so expertly cheated and those who begrudged the betrayal of their good faith. Pretence is one thing, it seems, false pretence quite another – even in a realm where fabrication and make-believe are understood to be the currency we deal in.

The audience in *Stage Fright*, on the other hand, were offered no structural alibi to account for the falsity of something they had witnessed for themselves. They were forced to negotiate between two forms of vision, a mendacious one and one whose veracity could be relied upon. And what Hitchcock wanted to understand was why this device would figure as such a fundamental breach of faith for the audience, so disrupt their sense of solidarity with a film that it could call into question the entire work. The failure of *Stage Fright*, Hitchcock suggested, derived largely from his failure to keep his side of an implicit compact with cinema audiences – that, unless explicitly told otherwise, it is safe for them to trust the evidence of their eyes.

And at one level the answer to his question is relatively simple. We can illuminate the matter by imagining the obvious alternative for incorporating misleading information into a film. Hitchcock could readily have presented his false past by means of a deliberately untruthful speech from one of his characters. But in that case the audience wouldn't have been intimately implicated in the falsehood. When it was revealed as such we would have known ourselves to be deceived, just as surely as we do in the existing film, but the lie would have been safely attached to that particular character. And this would have met with an expectation we carry always at hand. We understand, at some level, that strangers are potentially unreliable, and that nothing about language can offer an absolute guarantee of its truth, above all when language is detached from the thing it describes. Knowing that we have to take verbal accounts on trust, we reserve a small space in our minds for the possibility that trust will be betrayed.

But when the falsehood is presented directly to our eyes rather than our ears, our circumstances are altogether different. It's true that we know appearances can mislead too, but that isn't what is involved here. A film that ingeniously revealed that we had *misinterpreted* a sight, and that showed it to us again, unaltered by anything but an enlargement in our own perceptions, would probably offer a large satisfaction to the average viewer – not the discontented feeling of having been cheated in some way. There is a film, Francis Ford Coppola's *The Conversation*, that attempts to pull off this trick with sound, returning to an ambiguous phrase to reveal that it has been fatally misunderstood by the main character. But it is the disabling flaw of *The Conversation* that it has to cheat on its revelation – the sentence isn't the same at all, the intonation having been crucially altered. When first heard it is 'He'd kill *us* if he had the chance', the stress clearly implicating the two talkers in a plan of pre-emptive murder. When it returns the stress has disappeared, so that the sentence merely represents the expression of a fear.

The flashback in *Stage Fright* does something else altogether. It creates a situation in which, to restore the integrity of the film's storyline, we most discount the evidence of our own eyes, and in doing so it calls into question the supremacy of vision as the most reliable of our senses. Cinema also has ways of delivering compromised visions that don't bring about this sense of disruption – identifying unreliable sequences with the classic markers of fantasy or delirium. It doesn't even matter if the marker comes at the end of a passage, after we have been momentarily lulled into belief. Think of the countless dream sequences in the movies that snap from one category (really happening) to another (just a dream) with a single cut to a sleeper jerking from slumber. But Hitchcock had attached none of these signals to his flashback, nothing that would allow us later to acquit our eyes of the charge of collaborating in our deception. And in doing that he broke a cardinal rule of popular cinema: that we can rely on what we see. An art form that takes possession of our vision as utterly as cinema does has forced us to surrender control of the sense on which we are most dependent for our survival.

This book is about the pleasures of that surrender and, more specifically, about the way that cinema can exploit and play with our instinctive dependence on vision as a way of understanding the world. It is called *Watching* because I want to bring a particular kind of scrutiny to bear on the screen, one that is slightly perverse in its procedures, in that it looks past the ostensible content of films – the performances of actors and the unfolding storylines – at the shared ways in which all films act upon our eyes. The verb 'to watch' has a slightly curious status in the idiom of cinema-going. When someone asks you to accompany them to the cinema they are more likely, in Britain at least, to ask whether you want to 'see a film'. And 'seeing' is a word that usually implies a kind of passivity of reception. It's true that we also use it as a way of referring to mental understanding but, when used specifically of vision, 'seeing' is a kind of lowest common denominator, only one step above the most passive of all phrases – 'taking in a movie'. If our eyes are open, we will see something, whether we like it or not.

'Watching' is altogether more vigilant, a word that necessarily implies a narrowing of the field of vision. You can see a view, for instance, but you cannot – in English idiom at least – watch one, because your attention will need to be focused on some element within it. In that respect, 'watching' is often associated with a kind of tunnel vision: in order for vigilance to operate at all the watcher must, by an act of will, become blind to all kinds of peripheral and distracting detail. In addition, 'watching' usually contains a flavour of expectation, the sense of waiting for something to become manifest or change its nature, and that suits my purposes here, too, because these essays are partly about the subtle negotiations between the predictable and unexpected on which all cinema depends. And 'watching' often implies something else besides, a kind of wariness that presupposes a reason for caution. You watch for the expected arrival of an enemy or for an outbreak of fire and because of that it is easy for it to appear contrary or even hostile. It is to be on the lookout for something other than what the film intends us to see.

This is not a form of alertness that is always easy to maintain. It is liable to sedation, for instance, by the narcotics of narrative or beauty or psychological identification, which so easily destroy our sober detachment from a film. These are prejudicial terms, of course, though that hardly makes them unusual in the language of film criticism and theory, which often seems beset by a profound mistrust of their object of study, and a suspicion of the experience of pleasure. Many recent theoretical approaches can give the impression that the audience member is first of all a victim, played upon by sophisticated frauds and concealed acts of coercion and manipulation. Even the technical language incorporates the sense of criticism as an act of resistance to some conspiracy against our judgements. Noel Burch's description of the classic Hollywood narrative style as the Institutional Mode of Representation offers what appears to be a scientifically dispassionate language but is actually an arraignment in itself. At this end of the twentieth century we all know about institutions and what it is to be institutionalized. *The Cinema Book*, a standard textbook on Film Theory (and a good one, too) gives the game away when it talks of 'the narrative codes that were ultimately to constitute part of the armoury of the Institutional Mode of Representation'. Why 'armoury'? Because this is war and Hollywood is a superpower, against which the theorists are bound to mount a guerrilla resistance. Laura Mulvey, in an influential and much quoted article on 'Visual Pleasure and Narrative Cinema', is even more explicit: 'It is said that analysing pleasure or beauty destroys it. That is the intention of this article.' To be fair, she goes on to propose some consolations for her iconoclasm, but the general thrust remains one of puritanical reformation, the replacement of a popular religion, Technicolor in its ceremonial, with a kind of cinematic Jansenism.

The attempt to place cinema criticism on some sound scientific basis proved equally melancholy – an act of diagnostic surgery that almost always resulted in the death of the patient. While it is possible to understand the eagerness to replace a wine-sipping approach, in which personal connoisseurship and personal palate were the essential tools of criticism, the instruments laboriously forged by such theorists as Christian Metz never proved adequate to the task of establishing universal standards. To look at the evolution of Metz's '*grand syntagmatique*' is to watch a doomed attempt to reduce the irreducible. His prototype machine starts out with a certain elegance of design, but soon it is bristling with jury-rigged additions, each marking the recognition of a fresh problem, a new way in which the subject might escape the cage that is being built for it. It stands now as an impressive folly – a memorial to a laborious taxonomic enterprise that was never likely to succeed, any more than similar enterprises that borrowed their language from acts of biological dissection or chemical analysis or molecular science. This isn't to argue that cinema simply isn't susceptible to rational analysis, but it is to suggest that the peculiar nature of the art will always elude attempts to create a simplified grammar for its communication of meaning.

There was resistance to the resistance, of course, some of it positively quixotic in its nature. Barry Salt, a heretical outsider from the prevailing academic orthodoxies, reacted to what he saw as the pseudo-science of structuralism and semiotics by proposing a purified scientific approach. 'The serious study of the cinema should strive towards, without being able to attain, the nature of the established sciences such as biology and physics, which are identical in England and Russia, America and China,' he wrote in the preface to *Film Style and Technology*. That concessionary sub-clause, 'without being able to attain', begs a large question about whether the direction of striving is the right one. The problem with emulating the sciences in the field of cultural studies is that, while water boils at the same temperature in Russia, America and China, tempers don't, and it is out of such malleable and unquantifiable elements that cinema is constructed. Barry Salt identifies certain kinds of semiotic approach as being pseudo-science but he himself then makes the mistake of locating the error on the wrong side of the hyphen – it isn't that such attempts were faulty in their science but that they were scientific in the first place. More seriously, his attempts to outlaw subjectivity from the consideration of film result in an extraordinarily arid subjection of the audience to the intentions of the artist. 'By these standards,' he writes in the preface, 'a religious interpretation of a film on a non-religious subject by an irreligious film-maker would be regarded as invalid.'

I would want to disagree – or at least argue that 'invalid' is hardly a relevant term in such circumstances. And this is not just because one wants to substitute an 'anything-goes' subjectivity for a system of testable hypotheses. Scientific procedures are not, for the reasons I've just advanced, particularly good models for ways of thinking about cinema, but there are two areas of science that I think offer useful metaphors, as long as we bear in mind that metaphors are all they are. The first is chaos theory, with its central revelation that unpredictable complexity can be generated from relatively simple and predictable states. This seems to me pertinent to cinema, an explanation of why even the most rigorous theoretical analysis will never have any kind of predictive force. There are just too many intangibles in the equation, the greatest of them all being the psychology of the individual viewer. The second science is that of evolutionary theory, which I think offers a way of reconciling the liberty of individual audience members to feel whatever they feel in front of a film with some measure of the likely success of such ideas in a wider arena. By this way of thinking, it wouldn't be the 'validity' of a particular idea that mattered but its fitness for the environment into which it emerged. An evolutionary biologist does not have to worry about the truth content of a leopard – only about its position in a complex and changing ecological system. So, to take up Salt's particular example, it would not make sense to dismiss as 'invalid' an account of Hitchcock's *Notorious* that interpreted the film as an allegory for the Christian soul's hesitant approach to God (since such an account might have a large validity for a Jesuit film buff), but it would be reasonable to discuss its fitness in wider circumstances, the likelihood of it spreading and replicating itself in the greater environment of all those who watch *Notorious*. Of course, I might want to offer an argument that I thought stood a better chance of survival in that environment, but its success would depend on its ability to adapt to particular conditions, and even a changing intellectual climate. There are elaborately Freudian and Marxist readings of film, which now look considerably more embattled and endangered than they did twenty years ago, when they inhabited an academic ecology which favoured such ideas. (It's important to remember, I think, that this is just a metaphor; because the environment of those who watch and think about films is not remotely like any natural ecology. One important distinction would be that audiences are predisposed towards novelty, whereas Nature has no such prejudice.)

There's another respect, too, in which Darwinian theory might be useful for anyone who wants to understand the ways in which films work upon us, and that is at the level of our physiological responses to film. What remains consistent between a Bresson film and a Bruckheimer action picture (and there *are* viewers prepared to watch both) is the body of the audience – both in the sense of its collective presence in the cinema and the corporeal reflexes it brings into the cinema. Films are not shown to minds alone; they are shown to bodies that carry with them into the cinema all kinds of instincts and predispositions. Some of these are cultural and learnt, but many of them are inherited, and, without some acknowledgement of the way in which our vision is knitted inextricably into our sense of what it is to move through the world, we haven't properly begun to account for the ways in which films can affect us. I am not equipped even to offer a preliminary sketch of a coherent Darwinian aesthetic (and I suspect the exercise might offer fairly limited satisfaction anyway), but readers will find in the essays that follow references to the way in which our reflexes can be triggered by cinema. To put it another way, this is not a book that is suspicious of unthinking responses to film, since some of cinema's most powerful moments enlist our unconscious perceptual prejudices – including those vestigial impulses that were framed for very different conditions of life. To use the crudest example, I would suggest that our terror during scenes of stalking onscreen (an anxiety that often finds physical expression in the form of raised heartbeat and adrenalin release) is inseparable from our historic past as potential prey, however many layers of cultural reference and narrative coding have been laid on top.

As should be clear by now, this is not a work that sets out

to tidy up cinema, to make it less various and mysterious in its operations. That sense of a cheerfully unsystematic approach – one that does not feel the need for an underlying theoretical structure on which every idea depends – is reflected in the fact that it consists of six separate essays, none of which has any necessary relation to another. In writing the book and talking to others about it, I have often been asked why I chose these particular subjects and not others. The shortest answer to that is because these were the ones that intrigued me – as an ordinary cinema-goer who finds the perceptual sensation of cinema as important an element of its pleasures as the intellectual experience. A slightly longer answer would be that I wanted to find subjects that offered the opportunity to link a common and easily understood satisfaction of cinema with ideas that are more abstract and more theoretical. I hope the subjects for each essay are 'high-concept', to use a Hollywood pitching term. That is, they should be readily understandable, even for a drive-in audience. Nobody, I take it, will find the notion of an essay on the punch in film difficult to grasp, or the idea that 'making things big' is one of the cinema's unique contributions to our cultural experiences this century. Nor will they find it perverse to suggest that freeze frames are an element of film language that have a peculiar emotional force for viewers. But those relatively simple subjects, I think, conceal more complex matters that should be of interest to anyone who enjoys films. There are those who would argue that such enjoyment is incompatible with any kind of analysis – that the effortless education the movies give us in how movies work cannot be reconciled with an attempt to unpick the mechanisms that move us. I don't agree, partly because the combat between the screen and words is such an uneven one. However academic our scrutiny, however rigorous and focused our objectives, a screening of *Citizen Kane* still has the ability to make us forget what it was we came for. The arrival of video technology has changed this a little, making it possible for scholars to break the spell of unstoppable motion, to achieve in actuality the dissection for which critical language had so long appealed. But even on video, films will always win out over what is written about them.

More importantly, I don't believe that understanding is essentially inimical to pleasure. After an afternoon in the BFI Library, looking through back numbers of *Screen*, it isn't hard to see how such a prejudice might have arisen in this particular field. And though I have drawn on film theory in this book, I hope I have not been influenced by the conventional language of academic criticism, a dense and unforgiving medium that often seems to equate merit with impenetrability. That is a useful principle for the manufacturer of barbed wire but not for anyone who wants to share a pleasure with the reader.

The American humorist Will Rodgers once said: 'There is only one thing that can kill the movies and that is education' – and if you were to read only the more severe film theorists you might well decide that education would be perfectly happy to carry out the assignment. In truth, though, Rodgers was wrong – even in the sense he originally intended. Education cannot extinguish the dumb pleasures of the movies because they are designed to bypass the intellect anyway. It is my hope that this book will corrupt some innocent viewers, making conspicuous what had previously been transparent. But that corruption is intended to enlarge their pleasure, not diminish it.

BEGINNINGS

'When does the film start?' The question is almost bound to be straightforwardly functional, at least to begin with. You need to be in place, but you may not want to sit through twenty minutes of advertising, so you need a time of departure, a fixed point by which you will be in your seat and ready for the luminous transport of the screen. But the question is already marked by a tiny smear of anxiety. Like the question 'When does the train go?', it can still conjure in us the fretfulness of childhood – that age when we are always convinced that pleasure might leave without us. And when we are sitting in the cinema, when we have composed ourselves into an audience, and resolved our anxieties of eye-line and posture, the question remains, with a different note of frustrated eagerness. It means something else now: 'How long do we have to wait?' – a question that is not going to be answered by squinting at your watch, but by an ebbing of the light so imperceptible at first that you may feel your desire has duped your senses. Has impatience conjured that downward gradient of illumination or is it for real?

Even when dimming of the light is undeniable, the disquiet is still not entirely resolved. The question has taken on a larger scope, has become almost philosophical, and the audience is clearly not yet as one on the issue. Some accept the growing bulk of the darkness as a beginning in itself; others seem to take the view that a film only starts when they stop talking, a moment that may take some time to arrive. The disagreement escalates by practised degrees. First there is a turn of the head that fixes no particular individual (the gesture says only 'Where *is* that baffling noise coming from?', which is duplicitous – you know perfectly well – but it may preserve the peace). Then the look is levelled with more hostile accuracy and weight ('Some people have no manners!'). On rare occasions the engagement will even mount to a slushy hiss of disapproval from braver members of the silent majority. But even when the hushing has had its effect, when a kind of consensual silence has been reached and individuals surrender to a common feeling, we still have no absolute answer. Praising the celebrated single-take opening of Orson Welles's *Touch of Evil*, François Truffaut wrote with a casual perversity, 'All this happens before the film starts.' But when does the film start?

It should hardly need saying, first, that the starting point for a film as an artistic project may be very different from the starting point of the film as completed work. A director or writer may have been stimulated by some intimate provocation that will never explicitly feature in the film itself; the studio that puts up the money might have been encouraged by the box-office returns for a rival studio's surprise hit. So the start of a film, in that larger sense, may lie in a quarrel between a man and his wife or in the commercial statistics printed in *Variety* or in another film altogether. Nor is the chain of consequences likely to stop there. Where exactly in Steven Spielberg's life or the evolution of his personal ambitions could we confidently find the beginning of *Schindler's List*? After yet another disappointing Oscar ceremony? In a therapy session? In a call home to his father? Spielberg will have his own narrative of genesis to offer to journalists – those eager genealogists of projects – but even that will have to be artificially shaped as a story, with a fixed moment of initiation, from which everything else can follow. In life these beginnings are negotiable and subject to endless revision; in art they must be fixed with a precision that may not be true but has to be plausible. In the preface to *Roderick Hudson*, Henry James wrote this: 'Really, universally, relations stop nowhere, and the exquisite problem of the artist is eternally but to draw, by a geometry of his own, the circle within which they shall happily appear to do so.' James was writing about the predicament of conclusion, but his figure of a persuasive circle naturally encompasses beginnings as well.

This isn't simply a problem for the artist, either, because modern commercial practice has frayed the boundaries of commencement for an audience as well. We might equally ask ourselves when we truly first catch sight of a film. Is it when we watch the trailer that compresses its virtues (or vices) into a kind of dramatic pornography – all the climaxes without the relationships? Or is it when we see an interview with the star, interleaved with representative and, the studio must hope, seductive clips? Or even when we buy the cereal that contains a plastic model of one of its characters? It isn't uncommon now for viewers to have seen three to four minutes of a new film (even a notionally non-commercial film) before entering the cinema, and those clips will inevitably have taken precedence over the first frames you see, forcing them into some kind of subsidiary relation.* 'How do we get from here to that crucial explosion/kiss/slammed door?' you may find yourself thinking, unable to see the opening of a film as anything but a prelude to the dismembered scenes that have already secured your attendance. Aristotle wrote of beginnings in the *Poetics*: 'A beginning is that which itself does not of necessity follow something else, but after which there naturally is, or comes into being, something else.' The apparent simplicity of his description is deceptive – what appears to be starkly self-evident actually contains a crucial assumption about causation. The key words are 'of necessity' and 'naturally', both of which imply that discrete narratives will identify themselves by the solidity of the links that chain one event or deed to its immediate consequence. By this account a beginning is chained on one side only; it is a fictional loose end that allows us to trace a single path through the matted and entangled fibres of the world.

Aristotle's *Cinematics* would have to read very differently: 'A

---

*If the anticipation is intense, the pre-emptive glimpses can take on a life of their own as cinema. In the United States, audiences were reported to have bought tickets for screenings at which they knew the trailer for the fourth *Star Wars* film was to be shown, leaving the cinema without watching the main attraction. In Britain the trailer was given its own press screening.

beginning is that which is preceded by a multi-million-dollar prime-site advertising campaign, with simultaneous media promotional campaigns and merchandising tie-ins.' And the scale of those overtures (the publicity budgets for major Hollywood pictures routinely exceed the entire cost of making more modest films) means that the beginning of the film itself often has a task of reassurance to perform. The evolution of the pre-credit sequence is a complicated matter, having as much to do with a director's impatience to get to work on the audience's sensibilities as with commercial necessity, but it can't be entirely detached from the very large expectations routinely generated by advance publicity. In many cases now the pre-credit sequence is not there to prepare the ground for the film that follows, but to make an immediate delivery on the promises that have gone before. 'The opening is worth the price of admission,' writes a critic about De Palma's *Snake Eyes*, and in doing so he acknowledges the real ambition of a contemporary beginning. Those dazzling displays of just what the film can do offer a conclusion to the publicity campaign rather than a preamble to what follows.

Fortunately, we can escape from such epistemological fogs into the sharper definitions of projected light – to machinery that has an on–off switch as life and art do not. For many directors the onset of darkness is the formal dividing line between what is and is not cinema. It is part of the ceremonial of film, a rite that both announces and initiates. 'The collective hypnosis into which the cinema audience is plunged by light and shade is very like a spiritualist seance,' said Jean Cocteau in a 1946 speech. He later elaborated on that metaphor more than once in his writings (he was a theorist for whom a little was made to go a very a long way): 'Cinematography is a powerful weapon for making men sleep on their feet. The darkness of the theatre and the lunar glow of the screen are quite liable to produce the collective hypnosis exploited by Indian fakirs.' This won't do at all, or at least not if he has any kind of duration in mind. It is far too stupefied as a description of our film-watching sensibility, even for films as self-consciously narcotic as Cocteau's. Whatever suspension takes place in front of the screen it is rarely as passively suggestible as this. The image has an obvious connection with Cocteau's ambition, expressed in another of his favourite metaphors, that his own films should operate as a kind of seance, with the film-maker simply constructing a solid table and the audience required to do the turning, to summon messages from the other side. It isn't very surprising that Luis Buñuel should employ a similar metaphor, given his taste for oneiric liberties. 'Film seems to be an involuntary imitation of dream,' he wrote once. 'The darkness that gradually invades the auditorium is the equivalent of closing our eyes.' And this won't do, either, however appealingly woozy it sounds. Whoever remembered the beginning of a dream? It is part of their essential quality that we find ourselves among them and are wrenched from them, without a sense of beginning or ending.*

Cocteau and Buñuel's remarks do alert us, though, to the ritual nature of this passage through darkness. All cinema beginnings are a restoration of sight after its brief eclipse, and many directors guarantee that purifying transition from one kind of vision to another by running their titles over black, withholding any kind of image so that when it is eventually granted to us our gratitude or responsiveness will be all the sharper. We yield up our vision of our surroundings only to have it replaced – a word that conveys both its restoration and the fact that what we see is almost certainly divorced from where we are. The fact that there is an unmysterious mechanical explanation for this ritual – that cinema needs darkness to pull off its illusion of strength (it is all too easy to forget how fragile and weak a cinema image is when it has contrived to make itself the brightest thing in the room) – cannot exorcize its magic. And one of the effects of that restoration is to induce in us a temporary

---

*Films cannot enjoy this luxury, though some cinema-goers used to in the days of rotating screenings, coming in halfway through a film and staying until they had reached the point at which they entered.

state, not of hypnosis, but of almost transcendental generosity. You only rarely hear it said of a film that 'It was good but it had a disappointing start', and this is not simply because – contrary to the proverbial wisdom – last impressions have the privilege of erasing what goes before them. It is also because there is a period during which the film cannot put a foot wrong. It is a very short period in some cases, to be sure, but it always exists nonetheless. Verlaine's notion of the '*pointe assassine*' – that fatal moment in a creative work that murders artistic merit – is relevant here. All films begin in a kind of immunity to assault, armoured by our will that they should succeed. All those small anxieties and impatiences of waiting for a film to begin find their ease in the first few frames – and it will be some time before we have seen enough for new doubts to crystallize. A film will never be as free as it is in its opening seconds.

It's true that people do frequently say that a beginning is 'slow' or 'off-putting', but disappointing beginnings can be rehabilitated by what follows in a way that cannot simply be reversed for disappointing endings – they are far less likely to be excused by what has gone before. Time's arrow works in favour of commencement anyway, because of our human instinct to look ahead: we are far less likely to nag a storyteller with 'What happened before?' than we are with 'What happened next?'* Similarly, a bad beginning isn't perceived to have betrayed us to quite the same degree as a bad ending because a film is never incorrigible until it is finally over. Of course, it is true that we sometimes go to the cinema ready for trouble, on the lookout for incriminating evidence or an excuse for a fight, but it would still be difficult to declare hostilities too quickly. How could you be certain that the film wasn't going

*The latter question may well be a beginning of another story altogether, or even another film. Godard's *A Bout de Souffle* is usually said to have its source in an item François Truffaut saw in a Parisian newspaper, which he passed on to Godard as a promising subject for a film. But, writing in *Cahiers*, Godard himself identified another origin for his own film: 'The character played by Jean Seberg was a continuation of her role in *Bonjour Tristesse*. I could have taken the last shot of Preminger's film and started after dissolving to a title "Three years later".'

to wrong-foot you, to provoke a wild swing that would carry you off balance? Some films, indeed, begin with just such calculated deception. A trivial but witty example would be the beginning of *The Ipcress File*, which opens with everything depicted as a fuzzy blur. The indignation you feel at the indolence of the projectionist is wittily transmuted into pleasure at the acuity of cinematic vision when Harry Palmer finds his glasses and everything snaps into crisp focus.* A more profound case in point would be the teasing beginning to Hitchcock's *Family Plot* – evidence that the quality of an opening need not rest on the quality of the film that follows it. Hitchcock begins his story in the cab of a truck with Bruce Dern and Barbara Harris, who are arguing heatedly. Just as the details of their conversation are beginning to form into a comprehensible plot, Harris shrieks and Dern slams on the brakes. A reverse angle shows us that Karen Black, spotlit by the headlights, has walked directly across the path of the truck. The camera then peels off, with a beautiful movement of distracted attention, abandoning what we have taken to be the film's principal characters for this compelling stranger.†

*The possibilities of misdirection in these beginnings is evidence in itself of just how vulnerable and helpless the audience is at this point, how little they have to go on. When the original audiences for Stanley Kubrick's *2001* found themselves watching a primeval scene of combat between apes, their surprise that what had been purchased in good faith as science fiction appeared to be a study in pre-history may have amounted in some cases to dismay. But it would have been absurd to react too early to such a departure from expectation. Similarly, there must have been audiences for Brian De Palma's *Blow Out* who took that film's commencement as evidence that they had taken a wrong turn at the multiplex; what you see is a conspicuously cheesy slasher movie (which doesn't entirely rule out the possibility that it *is* a De Palma film), but this turns out to be a movie within the movie, one of the low-rent productions on which John Travolta is working as a sound technician. It is an additional layer to the joke that this apparent misdirection genuinely meshes with the climax of De Palma's film – since the unsatisfactory scream that Travolta rejects as unconvincing is ultimately replaced by the genuine scream of his murdered girlfriend.
†Attentive readers, or those with long memories, will realize that this is not the beginning of the film at all. There is, in fact, quite a long preamble before we arrive at this moment, involving fortune-telling and other forgettable nonsense. I leave the false recollection uncorrected because it offers a good example of the

It's worth bearing in mind that films may be a good deal more nervous than the audience at the moment of introduction. The audience has nothing to prove, after all, but the film most certainly does – above all, the fact that the cinema-goers are not wasting their time and money. This is particularly true of commercial cinema, which can rely less on our indulgence as viewers, and which is therefore obliged to pander to our desires, a compulsion that has damaged far more films than it has strengthened. The film may have some power over us, invested with authority by reason of its novelty as something to look at. But it is also dependent on our whim, our tyrannical ability to look away, to mock or to walk out, and it takes a strong nerve on the part of a director (or a studio) to resist the urge to seduce. It is also understandable if directors and producers want to secure our commitment as early as possible. As we shall see later, the dynamic of immediate nervous excitement, followed by an interlude of relaxation, grows in proportion to the financial risk involved in making a large-scale commercial picture. It also generates a kind of hysterical urgency about the speed of arousal. Sam Fuller is reported to have once said, 'When you start your script, if the first scene doesn't give you a hard on, throw the damn thing away.'*

But even if there is a tremor of supplication at the beginning of many films, it's still the case that this is the point at which authority can best be asserted, whether we mean by that term a public display of the creator's signature or a declaration of the temporary powers over our imagination that the film pro-

---

way in which a film's beginning can be a highly subjective moment – the audience may decide that things only properly get started long after the director believes he's set out. In the re-edited and truncated version of *Family Plot* that now plays in my memory this will always be the beginning. The plot structure for *Family Plot* recalls a trick played at much larger scale on the audience of *Psycho*, a film that swerves off the narrative highway it has already established down an unsurfaced side road. It is also an echo of a specific scene in the earlier film – that in which Janet Leigh's boss passes in front of her car at a pedestrian crossing and does a quizzical double-take when he sees her.

*In the television documentary *Typewriter, Movie Camera* about Sam Fuller.

poses to seize. And mastery, as any anthropologist could tell you, can be asserted in all kinds of ways – by enforced attendance (making the audience wait at the director's convenience), by ceremonies of admission (the long procession to the inner chamber) or by sheer intimidation (the filmic equivalent of the low chair, which places a nervous interviewee at an immediate disadvantage to the interviewer). In the best cinematic beginnings of all there will be something of all these techniques at work. Take *Touch of Evil*, for example. Here is one description of that celebrated initiation:

> The opening of *Touch of Evil* with its 'extraordinary' tracking shot has become a famous point of reference in 'film culture' and the 'breathtaking achievement' it represents is one element among many others which can be systematised in reading as the signature 'Orson Welles', the style of the author.

There are several things to note about this passage, part of 'Questions of Cinema', an essay by Stephen Heath,* which has itself become a famous point of reference in 'film studies'. The first of them would be what a note of fastidious distaste it sounds. It both includes and disavows the clichés it uses with those pinched inverted commas, profiting from their excitement but reluctant to touch them with bare hands. It will not stand by what it says, just in case that simplistic enthusiasm should prove contagious.

But Heath's essay finds other ways to pay tribute. His immensely detailed dissection of *Touch of Evil*, which dissects the film's volatile compound into separate elements, is a kind of obeisance in itself, however clinically disinterested its method. And he has undoubtedly picked his film wisely to bolster what he wishes to say about beginnings: 'A beginning, therefore, is always a violence, the interruption of the homogeneity of S' (S being the status quo that notionally prevails before the film begins). This is likely to strike us as particularly

---

*Published in *Screen*, vol. 16, nos 1 and 2.

plausible when the film under discussion begins with a single three-minute take that lays out the main components of the plot and welds them together with a terminal explosion – even more so when the manner of that shot so perfectly matches Heath's model of continuity and disruption, with the perceptual jolt of the first cut to a burning car after that long unbroken tracking shot. And, in so far as a beginning is only discernible as a beginning when it breaks the continuity of our perceptions, Heath must be right. His introduction of the idea of 'exhaustion' – in other words that the ending of the film must 'use up' the novel elements presented to the audience in the first place – is also convincing. It speaks directly to that dissatisfaction we feel with films that do not properly seal themselves from our world, that leave loose ends of speculation trailing into the light of day. (And if the film cannot resolve all of the uncertainties it creates, then it had better find some effective way to induce amnesia about the less important mysteries. Raymond Chandler famously confessed that he did not know who had killed one of the minor characters in *The Big Sleep*, but Howard Hawks directed with sufficient verve to overcome our bafflement, not to mention his own.)

One is bound to wonder, though, whether the beginning of *Touch of Evil* can usefully serve as a type for anything but itself – it is so strenuously, so conspicuously there to be noticed. Welles's presence as director on the film was something of a surprise both to the industry and himself (the result, if Charlton Heston is to be believed, of his own recommendation and a canny three-for-the-price-of-one deal by the studio, who agreed that Welles could rewrite the script and direct provided that he did it for his actor's salary). Welles knew that this might be his last chance to overcome the prejudices his talent had aroused. So this self-conscious beginning is also a fresh start, a statement that says something like 'I can work on your terms and mine too.' It is intriguing that when Robert Altman took on Welles at his own game, in *The Player*, he was facing similar difficulties, looking to rehabilitate his reputation with the green-light men of Hollywood.* And his own unbroken take, he has conceded in interview, is partly showing off, the sequence acting as a display case for the kind of complicated logistical management that money-men seek – the ability to make things turn up on time. 'But it's also part of the thing,' he continued. 'I want you to know that you're looking at a film.'

That self-consciousness is more fittingly aligned to the film's artistic ambitions, but the problem with Altman's long take, when set alongside the one that inspired it, is that it has no ticking clock. Nothing really drives it but Altman's pleasure in his achievement and it ends not with a bang but a whimper. More gravely, perhaps, it is ironically detached from the film that follows. Altman's scene creates a complicity between the audiences who recognize its origin and a director whose relationship with Hollywood might almost be read as a reprise of Welles's brilliant failure. So the scene offers a kind of self-contradicting statement – 'They don't make them like this any more (but manifestly I can)' – which alerts you to the self-contradicting statement of the film as a whole – 'Hollywood is now incapable of making intelligent entertainments (and here's one that proves it).' Welles's opening is animated by some of the same dynamics – an ebullient glee at what the machinery of cinema can be made to do. But much of its force derives from the way that it is, at the same time, a calling card for the director and an unassuming servant for his tale. *A Touch of Evil* is partially about the making of stories. Quinlan is a type of the author, an inventor of falsehoods that contain truth, as his dishonest framing of Sanchez is finally corroborated by a real confession. And Welles is surely aware that both the director and the crooked policeman share an interest in how to frame people. (David Thomson has written persuasively in his

*It is worth remembering that Hollywood studio executives had fewer problems with the idea of the auteur than some critical theorists. Hollywood was auteurist long before the term was invented. Audiences might well be indifferent to the director's name but producers never were, because authority covered such vital matters as control of financial spending.

book *Rosebud* about what a lacerating self-portrait Quinlan is, of the way in which Welles deliberately created a caricature of his own sagging departure from sleek and precocious youth.)

This combination of qualities – flamboyance and self-effacement – should be impossible, but the beginning of *Touch of Evil* achieves it, almost erasing its technical skill by the purity of its tension, and by the way it combines in us a painful awareness of limited time and an uncertainty about how quickly it is running out. We know that the clock is ticking because we have seen it set as the bomb is primed and placed in the car boot. But even though there are no edits into which the director might have compressed elapsed time – even though reel time is real time – we soon lose track of the seconds, so that each moment of proximity in the duet performed by the car and the walking couple offers a small crescendo of anxiety. It would be quite easy for an unalerted viewer to watch the scene without ever being aware that it is composed of a single flowing take. Indeed, even if informed viewers watch in order to trace the trajectory of the camera, the sequence can induce them to forget what they came for, so effective is it.

Such innocent perceptions of the scene are assisted by the fact that Welles's opening shot is, in one respect, profoundly conservative. If you had to categorize it within a classification of beginnings, it would fall into the largest grouping of all, a category that probably includes the vast majority of all cinema beginnings: that is, the establishing shot – in its most simple form nothing more than a photograph of the place in which the opening action is to occur. In one sense, this has something quite other than disruptive ambitions – what Heath character-izes as a violence against the established order. On the contrary, it immediately seeks to restore some equilibrium to an audience that has just voluntarily divorced its visual perceptions from its sense of propriation, that instinctive awareness of our own position, which helps us to locate ourselves in the world. To sever vision from sensation is a classic way to induce nausea, and many openings serve as a brisk response to the audience's first instinctive question in circumstances of disorientation – 'Where am I?' (a question that has acted as a shorthand for groggy dissociation countless times). The establishing shot tells you, and in doing so it creates a temporary stability, whatever unbalancing acts are to follow. It offers the equivalent of a prominent red arrow bearing the legend 'You Are Here' – whether you find yourself looking at a trail winding through sagebrush or the architectural canyons of a large city. What's more, the establishing shot is almost bound to locate you in a less tangible geography too – the well-mapped territory of genres and expectations. If you are going to navigate success-fully through the film, you need to know where you are setting out from, and most beginnings are happy to supply the infor-mation without any additional spin. Welles wasn't, but then the topography of his setting – a border town agitated by racial suspicions – is an actor in the drama, never simply the ground on which it unfolds.

What you never sense in *Touch of Evil* is what is often true of more conventional establishing shots: that they serve as a kind of optical dust-jacket for the film, a protective binding that will hold the treasured elements of the narrative apart from more mundane forms of vision. The establishing shot in its least interesting form – as a kind of throat-clearing reflex on the part of jobbing directors – is hardly even taken as part of the film itself, which is why it is so frequently overprinted with credits and titles, in a way that more privileged scenes could not con-ceivably be. And in such circumstances it can be difficult to feel that the film has truly begun until the furniture of announce-ment and accreditation has finally been cleared away. This moment of departure is even highlighted in some films. In *The Killing*, Stanley Kubrick accentuates the preliminary feel of his establishing shots of the racetrack by concluding them with a starter's bell. The ominous sostenuto of the opening music instantly gives way to location sound: 'They're off!' and so are we.

But even if the establishing shot is simply a protective

wrapping, it is likely to convey important information. You *can* judge a book by its cover, after all, particularly if you take the precaution of having an effective appeals system which will correct any miscarriage of justice. And in the hands of capable Hollywood directors the welcoming signage of genre pictures could always be made to do a little extra work. Howard Hawks's sagebrush landscapes, often bisected by single wagon trails, served as both a trademark and an effective evocation of the Western's penetrative drama. The famous opening to John Ford's *The Searchers* locates the drama in Monument Valley, but moves towards it out of a surrounding blackness. The thrill of the moment at which that frame disappears and the landscape fills the screen is calculated to instil a shock of transition. Then out of that intimidating vastness advances a single man apparently at ease with his surroundings.

What the opening to *The Searchers* establishes, in addition to the arena in which the action is to unfold, is a mood. For most viewers it will offer a kind of preliminary instruction in how we are to approach the story (a protocol, if you like, and one quite as elaborate in its codes as those governing any diplomatic exchange). You don't have to interpret that black border consciously as a blazon of mourning to feel the ambiguity of the movement forwards – the tension it creates between interior and exterior. Are we being pushed unwillingly or pressing forward eagerly? (Martha, whose back we see, moves at a pace that will confirm neither hypothesis.) Is that black space a shelter or a trap? (It is unmistakably shown as the latter during the first Indian attack, when the sealing of the cabin windows delivers a claustrophobic flutter of panic.) Is the outside a place into which we can escape or a threatening void, a bare ground from which the messages of human permanence are continuously being erased?*

*In his book, *Signs and Meaning in the Cinema*, Peter Wollen says of this film: 'We are confident that the homesteader's wife, Mrs Jorgensen, is right when she says: "Some day this country's going to be a fine good place to be." The wilderness will, in the end, be turned into a garden.' In fact we are confident of no such

Of course, all these questions are deeply coloured by having seen what follows and a doubt might arise in the mind – is it really plausible that such a short sequence, only around fifteen seconds long, contains all that? We can perform a rather unsatisfactory thought experiment here (unsatisfactory because it is impossible to create any kind of respectable controls): what would happen if you stopped *The Searchers* after Ethan's first words and asked a cinematically literate but first-time viewer to interpret what they had seen? It wouldn't be impossible for an innocent watcher to guess at some of these themes, but for most people the scene would surely look more functional and matter-of-fact. They would be absorbing too much from the centre of the scene (metaphorically as well as literally) to be able to pay much attention to its periphery. So discussion would be liable to gravitate to technology – the exact nature of Ford's tracking shot, the difficulties, perhaps, of filming into that searing sunshine – rather than the narrative implications of his opening. It is only on a second viewing (or with a viewer already deflowered by critical paraphrase) that the full extent of the scene's meaning can possibly reveal itself. And the word 'implication' – with its etymological origins in the idea of a folding in – is instructive in understanding how this can work, how a sequence can be both plain and richly ornamented. The language of clarification is unusually attracted to the idea of a surface without concealing pleats or wrinkles. The way in which we talk of explication and explanation (from *explanare*, to make smooth), about how a story 'unfolds' or 'turns out', all hint at the idea that every element of a story is in some way present from the beginning. It may appear to be a critical con-

thing. American audiences knew, consciously or not, that Monument Valley was not a garden but a National Park. In other words, that Ford's scenery rested precisely on the failure of a civilizing project. The land had not been improved – in nineteenth-century terms – or spoiled – in terms of the century that preserved it. And Ford's film is animated by an explicit recognition of the land's victory – 'this God-forsaken wind scour', as Laurie puts it. In other words it isn't because of the successes that America honours its pioneers but because of all those unhonoured failures. *The Searchers is* a patriotic film, but never as complacently as Wollen makes out.

juring trick to unpack so much from that opening sequence, but the fact that we can demonstrates one of the necessary qualities of a truly great beginning – the sense that it is a bud from which the full bloom of the film will naturally unfurl.

'A beginning is often that which is left behind,' notes Edward Said in his book *Beginnings: Intention and Method*. It's an Aristotelian truism that repays some thought. (It reminds us, for one thing, that it can be hazardous for a beginning to be so memorable that it prevents our attention from moving on. All narratives depend on our restless infidelity to the moment just passed.) But it is also true – at least under modern conditions of consumption – that a beginning is that which is returned to. And here the great beginning demonstrates its powers of reinvention. Beginnings have an advantage over endings in this. They are more susceptible to revision on a second viewing. This is true even of a genre as liable to depletion as horror, where many of the effects will depend on the audience's ignorance and fearful misconstructions. The opening to Kubrick's *The Shining*, a sustained helicopter shot that follows the Torrances' small blue Volkswagen as it winds up the road to the Overlook Hotel, is a familiar kind of establishing shot, one that suggests a progression to the site in which the drama will be played out, and also compresses the extent of wilderness within which the characters are to be isolated. (The sometimes tedious duration of the title credits works to Kubrick's advantage here, in a sequence where time elapsed is also a measure of distance travelled. Indeed, it is possible to wonder whether he would have been able to run the sequence at quite such length without the accompanying alibi of the credits themselves, which usefully disable whatever impatience we might feel at the long deferment. There is some connection between scenes we feel entitled to talk over in the movies and scenes that the makers themselves feel entitled to write over.)

We are prejudiced viewers the first time we see this image. We are likely to know much about the film already, either from publicity or because we know what Stephen King novels are about generally. Even if we don't, the music effectively prohibits some responses – it instructs us that we should be looking for omens. And the position of the camera is the most obvious omen available; high and behind the object that it tracks, it has a predatory command. Had the car been filmed from in front, in view of its 'eyes', the sense of vulnerability would have been greatly diminished. Brief moments of escape, when the car plunges into a mountain tunnel or takes a sudden bend, prove to be illusory. The attention of the camera does not stray to what is conventionally 'spectacular' – the astonishing scenery all around – but remains inexorably fixed on that small (and peculiarly *protectible*) vehicle. There are other grace notes delivered by Kubrick's consistency here: his decision not to cut to different angles or views (from the inside of the car, for instance); most powerfully, perhaps, the almost subliminal insinuation made by the fact that all the other cars encountered on the road are travelling in the other direction. The Torrances are seen to be going the wrong way from the very opening frames. But a second viewing of *The Shining* does not diminish the effect of this beginning; indeed, it sharpens its effects because we know what is being travelled towards. The film has corroborated our initially unspecified disquiet and the opening sequence now serves as a *memento mori*.

Something similar happens to the beginning of Nicolas Roeg's *Don't Look Now*, a showcase opening that, on first encounter, immerses viewers in a pool of signs we have little hope of properly comprehending. The first time you see the red dye spreading from the damaged slide that Donald Sutherland is examining is a moment full of foreboding, certainly, but it cannot yet be read as fatal (unless you are yourself a psychic). And even though the cinema audience is bound to make connections between that image and the spreading crimson of the girl's raincoat as she drowns in the garden, we may not connect them as directly as the film has in mind. This may look like pattern-making on the part of the director, an aesthetic invention of symmetries rather than a record of a moment of prescience.

On a second viewing, though, our consternation and Donald Sutherland's diverge in a way that exacerbates the anxiety we feel. We now know precisely what this sequence has to say – that it *is* a communication. Sutherland does not, and is condemned to repeat his tragic hesitation as often as the film is run. So although the film is no longer a mystery to us – we have seen its workings – it has evolved into a different kind of thriller, one of preventable tragedy. And memory being as suggestible as it is, as ready to accept later revisions, it is often only when we go back and look knowingly at the beginning of a film that we are able to see with any clarity just how good a premonition it has given us for what follows.

This sense of the beginning as a suggestive epigraph for the film that follows is important to any aesthetics of commencement. Saul Bass, the most famous designer of credit sequences, once described the purpose of his titles as being to 'project a symbolic foretaste of what is to come, and to create a receptive atmosphere that will enable the film to begin on a higher level of audience rapport'. It's true that there is a faint whiff of oppression in these words – what is a receptive atmosphere precisely? It sounds as if a sedative might have been introduced into the air-conditioning, quelling whatever habits of dissent or resistance the audience have brought with them. Has the audience been seduced into happy compliance with the film's purposes or simply been made vulnerable to its pleasures? It needn't be sinister to say of Bass that he had designs on his audience – he was, after all, a designer who also worked in the commercial field – but there is nonetheless something invasive about the rhetoric he uses to describe his work. For Bass, it was important that the film secure a beachhead immediately. He wanted his titles to control the space that had, traditionally, been a kind of demilitarized zone.* As Bass pointed out in an interview with a design magazine:

Normally the running of the title is a period during which

---

*This metaphor may well have been provoked in me by the fact that *The Desert Fox*, Henry Hathaway's 1951 film about Rommel, is sometimes cited as being the first film to use a true pre-credit sequence. It wasn't quite – *Destry Rides* the patrons leave their seats for popcorn, make small talk with their neighbours, or simply explore their seats for long-term comfort, and when the film itself begins, there is usually an initial 'cold' period.

By this account, the credit sequence has to serve as a warm-up man for the headline act, chivvying the audience to stretch the affective muscles they will need in the next few hours. But there are less seductive purposes too. On another occasion, Bass said:

A show should start the moment the lights go down. The credit title should help fix an audience in its seats by creating a sense of atmosphere and a kind of expectation, get them quiet and in an interested mood right away.

In other words, the purpose of a film's beginning is to bring the audience to attention, eyes front. Obedient to the old disciplinary adage, masterful directors will begin as they mean to go on.

The question of title sequences undoubtedly complicates matters here. As an auteur of inauguration, Bass has a strong motive for incorporating his work within the entirety of the film, rather than merely antecedent to it. What's more, it is virtually impossible to think of *Psycho* without thinking of his graphic title sequence and the stabbing anxiety of Bernard Herrman's score. But that passage of intersecting lines is operating more as a pre-curtain overture than a true commencement. When does the film start? Surely with Hitchcock's long shot of the city – an image that allows us very briefly to dismiss it as innocuous, as a stock establishing shot, before it reveals its dynamism, advancing steadily to take us into the room where Janet Leigh is dressing after illicit sex (a voyeur's fantasy of city

---

Again delays the first title until about a minute into the film – but it was still rare enough to be remarked on by *Variety* in its review: 'Picture gets off to an unusually sock opening, depicting the November 1941 raid on Rommel's North African headquarters by British Commandos. This all takes place before the title and credits are flashed.'

life, in which every window might repay a stare).* It is Hitchcock's shot that sets the game rolling . . . but then Hitchcock's shot wouldn't look the same at all without Bass's grating prelude, which governs the ways in which we can look at this banal urban vista.

The matter becomes even more complicated when it becomes common practice to interleave a credit sequence with filmed elements of the story, as happens in *Casino*, where Bass's titles intersect with Martin Scorsese's opening footage to create a single entity. It isn't seamless, exactly – you can tell precisely where graphics takes over from photography – but no useful purpose would be served by dissecting one from the other. The opening images accelerate you from sartorial comedy (Scorsese emerging from the casino like a polyester flamingo) to the engulfing flame of explosion in the space of just a few seconds, and Bass's credits then maintain the pace, spinning De Niro's body through a purgatory of neon and fire. These frames make a large claim for the film that follows, amplified even further by the use of Bach's *Requiem* on the soundtrack. Not every viewer felt the promise of the opening had been made good by the end of the film, but it undoubtedly achieves what it sets out to do – to serve as a propellant that will kick us into the film before we have time to brace ourselves for its effects.†

Indeed, the beginning of *Casino* could be viewed as a shock-

---

*The establishing shot is sometimes useful *because* it is boring. To offer a trivial example, the beginning of *Die Hard with a Vengeance* at first appears to deliver a standard New York postcard opening – city streets, the Manhattan skyline, people descending into subways – and it is just as you are beginning to fret at the inertia of this opening (particularly when compared to the extravagant display we expect from big-budget stunt movies) that the film delivers its money shot – the sight of an entire city block exploding without warning, cars flipping into the street.

†I would suggest that *Casino* offers a classic case of a film unfairly cast into shadow by its predecessors. Had it come before *GoodFellas* in Scorsese's filmography it would have been recognized as the more serious and complex work, rather than the enervated repetition that some critics detected. In this respect, *Casino* offers an example, within the work of a single director, of how difficult it can be for a film to make a clean start.

ingly speeded-up version of Welles's canonical inception – location, character and inaugurating explosion in the space of just a few seconds. As in *Touch of Evil*, the explosion offers a narrative mystery ('a violence', if you like) that the film explicitly offers to resolve – because, unless Scorsese is playing the same game that Billy Wilder did in *Sunset Boulevard*, De Niro's voice-over assures us of his survival. It is a dark joke, too, that the lead character should turn the ignition key for his own story. The structure is one that is extremely familiar from film noir. Think of all those movies that begin with death and loop backwards to trace the inexorable movement towards a fate already known – the noose of the film's story-line pulling tight through the knot tied by the opening scene. But here Scorsese adds a kinetic impetus that he has made his own trademark. The beginning of *Mean Streets* comes to mind at once, that wonderful and canny syncopation by which Harvey Keitel's dream of judgement is followed by the title sequence, with its compelling sense that we have stumbled into a party that is already under way and, perhaps, a little out of control.

Certainly, speed in an unrefined form has always been a useful drug for a director to administer to an audience as the film begins. In *Performance*, for example, Nicolas Roeg and Donald Cammell opened their film with what I take to be a piece of found footage from a camera strapped to an experimental rocket. What you see is a vapour trail unreeling at immense speed into blue sky, but what you feel is a force of sheer acceleration. It's impossible to place this wild image into any coherent relationship with the story that follows, except that incoherent, hallucinatory thrust is obviously relevant to the film's story-line. Just as the film cut from this inexplicable symbol to an aerial shot of a Rolls-Royce (an image that *was* part of the narrative universe of the film), so Danny Boyle began his slickly efficient black comedy *Shallow Grave* with a speeded-up bumper-level tour of Edinburgh streets. What follows is essentially a chamber piece, played out in the confines of a spacious flat, so this topographical hustle has no structural

23

purpose within the film. You do not need it to comprehend what follows and it does not stand in metaphorical relationship to it. What it delivers is a visual 'rush', amphetamines in the form of light which leave the audience a little breathless and open to suggestion. (Boyle followed almost exactly the same tactics in *Trainspotting*, where the action begins in mid-flight as Renton pelts from a shop in which he has been caught stealing, although the scene here does have a direct connection with the film's storyline. It also conveys a subtly different message to the viewer: this film, like the people depicted in it, doesn't intend to stop for respectable passers-by.) In such openings we recover the older meaning of 'start' – a time when it meant to move with a sudden leap or outrush from a period of rest. In English, at least, 'start' is a word in which ideas of commencement and sudden impulse are inextricably bound.*

There is always a risk at such moments of leaving your audience behind, but directors can usually depend on our anxiety to keep up. There is a potent seduction in indifference, anyway, so that a film that does not pause to acknowledge your arrival has its own distinctive allure. In Patrice LaConte's *Ridicule*, the film opens with the audience trailing at the coat-tails of an unknown figure, whose unstoppable charge along a series of eighteenth-century corridors is viewed from behind and at calf-level. He turns out to be on his way to urinate copiously over a man who has mocked him, a splashy destination which more than justifies the sense that we are mere hangers-on, attendants at some ceremony that was not originally intended for our eyes. Other directors have assaulted the viewer's *amour propre* even more directly – most famously Samuel Fuller, who strapped an Arriflex camera to his camera-man's chest and then had Constance Towers whale at him with a high-heeled shoe until the wig slipped from her bald head. There can be few films that so explicitly come at the audience

---

*In the age of sail, to 'start' a crewman meant to sting him into action with a rope's end, a form of encouragement that some film-makers are also happy to employ.

and the effect is sufficiently startling to numb your critical responses for some time – after which it may become clear that *The Naked Kiss* is a film in which the distinction between brutal crudity and subversive melodrama is not always very clear. There are other films, too, that literally hit the ground running: Robert Aldrich's *Kiss Me Deadly*, for instance, which opens with a retreating tracking shot of a terrified, half-naked woman running down a desert highway.

This is not a cinematic invention, of course. *In medias res* has a long and distinguished literary history as a means for breaking and entering into a reader's imagination. But at first glance it might look as if there is a crucial difference between literature and cinema in respect of beginnings. After all, written narratives need, first of all, to establish some ground of trust between us and the author. The reliability of any literary description is an untested quantity and depends on the trust-worthiness of the human observer, who may well be a character within the novel and may, moreover, be there precisely to be proved wrong. Films, on the other hand, appear to take at least one step away from such anxieties. We are the observers, and we are unlikely to question the evidence of our own eyes, surely?

In practice, though, such distinctions are much more fragile than they might appear (and have become even more so as computer-generated imagery improves its deftness at forging what we once took to be the unfakeable authenticity of the visible world). The apparently all-important concordance between real objects and final film image is very quickly buried beneath the landslide of choices open to the director, actor and camera operator. It has become a commonplace to note how 'cinematic' some literary beginnings are. (Sergei Eisenstein takes exactly this approach when writing about Dickens's short story *The Cricket on the Hearth*, which he construes as a kind of establishing montage, made up of alternating close-ups and master shots.) But it is often forgotten (though not by Eisenstein) that this might equally well be a way of saying how 'literary' cinema remains. And at such points it becomes clear that the novel's devices are, in all essential points, much the same as cinema's. (That this is subconsciously acknowledged by film-makers is evidenced by the familiar cliché of turning pages for the title sequence of so many Hollywood films – which may even exceed those that have been adapted from well-known novels, where the device serves as a coded acknowledgement that the film has essentially illustrative status. These days the dominant trope for title sequences has changed from books to heavy machinery – to a booming metallic clang reminiscent of industrial steam hammers or slamming prison doors. How many Hollywood money machines now begin with this Dolby-boosted fanfare of epic status, the titles slamming into place on the screen to the grinding percussion of an immovable object meeting an unstoppable force? Cinema, it suggests, does not bust blocks any more by finding the way to a crack in your resistance, but by sheer ponderous weight.)

When Stendhal begins *Scarlet and Black* (a novel for which the epigraph is 'Truth – Truth in all her rugged harshness', a photographic motto before its time), his first sentence is this: 'The little town of Verrières is one of the prettiest in Franche-Comté.' What follows is a subtly mediated gazetteer entry, blending topography, history and commercial information (there is even an allusion to the 'traveller', the imagined figure for whom this information has been assembled). This beginning would be easy to replicate on film as a conventional establishing shot – a long shot for the 'white houses, with their red-tiled, pointed roofs', moving on to a montage of medium shots of the 'saw-mills busily whirring' and the pounding hammers of the nail factory as well as close-ups of feminine hands 'placing the little bits of iron beneath these hammers'. But in any scene-for-sentence transcription it would end up looking very much like a geographical information film, taking in the town's historic sights ('fortifications which were built up centuries ago by the Spaniards') and its principal industries.

Film is naturally capable of similar masquerades. In fact, what Stendhal's opening brings to mind – at least in its use of an idiom at odds with fictional manners – is the celebrated beginning of *Citizen Kane*, a knowing game with cinematic conventions of fiction and truth. The film famously begins with an ending – which turns out to be both that of its main character and of the film itself – because at the conclusion the opening shot is almost exactly reversed (with some economies of time), pulling back from the spectral silhouette of Xanadu (now uttering black smoke from the cremation of Rosebud), slowly down the wire-fencing to pause on the 'no trespassing' sign which was the very first thing we saw (initially Welles's impudent reminder of how comprehensively the film had evaded Hearst's security measures, but now a sign that somehow also acknowledges the impenetrability of death). The mood at the beginning is almost absurdly Gothic.*

But those genre mysteries are very soon dispelled by a second beginning, when the strident simplifications of the news on the March newsreel shatter the mood of gloomy reverie. This, too, is a combative gesture against Hearst, every frame confirming the rumours about the film's real subject. Even the protective line 'How was he any different from Ford . . . or Hearst for that matter . . .?' is confrontational, an assertion of identity that cheekily takes the form of a disclaimer.

David Thomson says about the pre-newsreel section of *Citizen Kane* – the mist and montage section – that 'it's teaching us how to know it'. His point is that the medium of film is here made so opaque and conspicuous that we can barely see through it to the story it should be conveying. 'No American film took such chances with entertainment's ground rules,' he adds, arguing that you are some way into *Kane* before it becomes clear what you, as viewer, should care about. But I think this is

*The first time I saw *Citizen Kane*, as a child aware only of its cinematic reputation, I took it to be a horror story and, being alone and rather impressionable, became so nervous about what might lie behind that single lighted window (which has an eerie stability through the approaching montages, not even shifting its position onscreen when the castle is inverted by the reflection in the gondola lake) that I switched off the television and went to bed. In other words, the first time I saw *Citizen Kane* I didn't see it at all.

to miss how cannily Welles blends invention with convention. The dissatisfaction of the newsreel editor announces with quite audacious clarity both where the story is (Kane's life) and where it isn't (the public, official biography). *Citizen Kane* is a quest and the terms of the quest are laid down quite explicitly at the beginning. In that sense it is not a film that takes any large risks with the impatience of its audience. You would have to be extraordinarily peremptory to insist on clarification so soon, particularly when the promise conveyed by Welles's combination of horror style and newsreel is so intriguing – a monster movie with a difference. That the film was not a hit at the time of its first release is really evidence not of the wariness of American audiences but of the effective rearguard bullying action mounted by Hearst and his supporters. *The Magnificent Ambersons* was more reckless in this regard, beginning with fifteen seconds of blackness and the long preamble of Welles's narration, which reduced the film itself to the status of illustration. It suffered accordingly for its daring.

But Thomson's recognition that original films must incorporate some kind of tuition within their very structure is important. I used the word protocol earlier to describe the opening sequence of *The Searchers*, a word that now has the sense of a formal agreement of terms (whether it's between diplomats or fax machines), but which in the original Greek described the flyleaf or first page of a manuscript, often glued to the scroll case and containing an account of its contents. Many films use such protocols to bring us into alignment with their intentions, sometimes without any element of diplomatic concealment. The tendency of French films to open proceedings with a formal epigraph or even a direct address to the viewer is one obvious case in point. The first photographic frames of *La Règle du Jeu* are preceded by an instructive title card: 'This story is intended as entertainment, not social criticism', a warning note tendered to the more earnest French film-goer, always prone to leap to political conclusions. The admonition can run in the other direction too. Robert Bresson's *Pickpocket* begins with this stern and detailed announcement:

> Ce film n'est pas du style policier. L'auteur s'efforce d'exprimer par des images et des sons le cauchemar d'un jeune homme pousse par sa faiblesse dans une aventure de vol à la tire pour laquelle il n'était pas fait. Seulement cette aventure, par des chemins étranges, reunira deux âmes qui, sans elle, ne se seraient peut-être jamais connues.*

This preliminary paraphrase is in keeping with Bresson's assiduous exclusion of narrative tension from his films (Susan Sontag has noted how the title alone of *Un Condamné à Mort s'est Échappé* effectively removes all uncertainty about the outcome of the film). But it also betrays the anxiety of a director faced with the crudity of his audiences' appetites. In its implied disdain for the '*style policier*' there is something reminiscent of a maître d' advising an unsuitable-looking client that Coca-Cola is *not* served in his establishment. Any alert viewer would soon realize that Bresson's film is not a genre exercise, but the formal instruction counters any complaints before they arise.

This rather Gallic strain of solemnity about a film's proce-dures (a solemnity that need not exclude wit, incidentally) also finds expression within the film itself, rather than solely in the anteroom of the titles.† The beginning of Godard's *Le Mépris*,

*'This film is not a "policier". The author has attempted to express by images and sounds the nightmare of a young man pushed by his own weakness into an adventure of pickpocketing for which he was not made. Only this adventure, by a strange route, reunites two souls who, without it, would perhaps never have known each other.'
†It is not *exclusively* Gallic, of course. Hitchcock had actually delivered a rather similar prologue to the audience at the beginning of *The Wrong Man*, released two years before *Pickpocket*. Hitchcock's film opens with the director's silhouette addressing the audience and explaining that 'this film is unlike any of my other films. There is no suspense. Only the truth.' *Ce film n'est pas du style policier*, in other words. And this kind of direct instruction can take indirect forms. The opening of Spike Lee's *Malcolm X* employs a self-consciously inflammatory rhetoric to introduce its biography of the black leader. One of Malcolm X's

in which the physical machinery of the tracking shot is displayed
(by a tracking shot) before you see *another* tracking shot made
with that very machinery, is clearly a similar insistence that we
should bring specific kinds of attention to what we see. It
informs us that this is a film about cinematic observation, as
Godard later confirmed in *Cahiers du Cinéma*:

> The point of *Le Mépris* is that these are people who look at
> each other and judge each other, and then are in turn looked
> at and judged by the cinema ... Whereas the *Odyssey* of
> Ulysses was a physical phenomenon, I filmed a spiritual
> odyssey: the eye of the camera watching these characters in
> search of Homer replaces that of the gods watching over
> Ulysses and his companions.

There are, naturally, less dominating forms that instruction can
take, something closer to courtesies of greeting or information
than a stern induction. The independent film-maker John Sayles
describes the opening of his science-fiction film *Brother from
Another Planet* in just such terms:

> In the first five minutes of the movie we have some purposely
> very tacky special effects to say 'Folks, this isn't *Star Wars*.
> This is a $1.98 universe you've walked into. This is about
> the character and not about the special effects.' That thing
> of letting people know what world they've entered is some-
> thing that I try to do in every film.

The famous opening of Hitchcock's *Rear Window* offers
another notable example. Most people have little difficulty in
remembering the exemplary narrative economy of the pan

---

arraignments of white America is accompanied by a montage that includes the
burning of the American flag and clips from the Rodney King video in which a
black motorist was recorded being savagely beaten by white police officers. The
sequence tells you not only that this is a film about rage, but that the historical
anger described has not yet outlived its purpose – it is the celluloid equivalent of
throwing a Molotov cocktail into the auditorium, a provocation to feelings
of prejudice from both black and white audiences that the film then sets out to
explore.

across the photographer's shelving, a brief sequence that crisply informs you what he does, how he has been injured and the nature of his relationship to Grace Kelly. But people often remember this incorrectly as the beginning of the film. In fact, Hitchcock opens with a curious and entirely non-naturalistic unveiling, in which the blinds of the picture window in front of which Stewart sits for his entertainment are rolled up, one by one, and with a tantalizing protractedness. This is a curtain-up and it establishes the space behind as a dramatic spectacle, a space that is toured by Hitchcock's camera in a visual equivalent to the introductory cast list. This, too, is a masterpiece of narrative brevity, a moving Advent calendar in which each aperture gives us the caricature of a life. The instructions here vary in their register – from the straightforward pre-emption of obvious questions to the far subtler announcement of the film's theme of judgement by appearance (it is not watching people that is a sin in *Rear Window*, but judging on the basis of inspection alone).

So where does all this end? We can hardly conclude, I think, with any useful taxonomy of beginnings, nor any stable prescription for good practice. For one thing, a beginning, however politely it respects the existing conventions and however solicitously it considers our sensibilities, will always be as concerned with breaking rules as with honouring them – Edward Said notes pertinently that the Arabic word for heresy is synonymous with the verb 'to innovate' or 'to begin'. Beginnings are always a kind of departure from precedent, so precedents can have no general application. For another thing, a beginning's virtues cannot properly be judged apart from what succeeds it. 'A beginning is an artifice,' writes Ian McEwan in his novel *Enduring Love*, 'and what recommends one over another is how much sense it makes of what follows.' This is, necessarily, an account of retrospective judgement. It raises the paradox of all beginnings – that we can only confidently approve of their means when we know to what end they are proceeding – and yet by that time the beginning itself may be out of reach, in the past. (In this respect the gap between the screen, where the beginning must be effaced by what comes next, and print, in which the beginning is always close at hand, has been narrowed by the arrival of video but still not entirely closed.) In any case, as we've seen, cinematic beginnings often have duties other than 'making sense' of what follows; they may be required simply to arouse us or realign our perceptions into a mood of appropriate susceptibility.

But it should be possible to describe the qualities of a great beginning, as opposed to a merely enjoyable one, and McEwan's remark is useful here. It reminds us that a great beginning is inextricably connected to the body of the film, is never just a bravura display of energy or flair but always an integral part of the whole. A great beginning has a prescience to it that we cannot consciously recognize on first encounter and that reveals itself only by degrees. As a result you might say, paradoxically, that a great beginning reveals itself not by the qualities of its own initiation but by the difficulty we have in saying precisely where it ends and the rest of the film takes over. Such beginnings are rare in cinema, and worth treasuring, but their rarity may not ultimately matter, given the aura of invulnerability that surrounds a film in its opening minutes, when the romance of watching is fresh within us. So many of the obvious charges we might bring against a film are inadmissible at this point. The opening frames of a film cannot be meaningless, because their obscurity may be a meaning in itself; they cannot be a non sequitur because they have nothing to follow; they cannot be dull because they are so bright in comparison with the gloom that preceded them. In this, every new film offers a recapitulation of our experience of all films – beginning in uncritical innocence and only slowly acquiring the potential for doubt and discrimination. Whether it is a great beginning or a terrible one, the opening shots of any film are our moments of purest speculation in the cinema, a time when our curiosity about the film and our pleasure in looking at it are perfectly aligned.

THE PUNCH

It can sometimes seem as if there has never been a time when cinema wasn't spoiling for a fight. The very earliest fragments of cinema – mere protozoa of projected light, flickering on tacked-up sheets in hastily converted shop fronts – were prone to sudden eruptions of violence. Take this reminiscence of a Philadelphia 'moving photograph' show of the 1890s:

> After a few minutes of this luminous orgy . . . a man's face popped out from between two brilliant splotches of light. Soon, another face appeared in the northwest corner of the sheet. Later, a human torso flashed into view; then its arms popped into place, then its legs; its head arrived soon after, and it stood revealed in its entirety – a perfect man. Eventually he was joined by his pal. For nearly a minute they gestured and gesticulated at each other. Finally Number One lost his temper. Without warning he launched a vicious blow at Number Two. Whether the blow was a knockout I shall never know. Before it landed, the sheet was plunged into pitchy darkness – and the show was over.*

There is a mysterious poignancy in that unlanded blow, a withheld satisfaction that cinema was to make good many thousands of times in the succeeding decades. Why was it thrown in the first place? The setting is so sparse and so indifferent to psychological coherence that it seems almost absurd to ask questions about motive. Film is still a technology at this point, not yet a medium. But it's tempting to project a meaning on to the image, to throw our own light on to this prehistoric fragment of cinema. And it would surely involve some combination of fear and frustration on the part of those who had filmed the scene. At a loss to the larger potential of the camera, troubled

*The Parade's Gone By, Kevin Brownlow, University of California Press, 1983.

by what André Bazin called the 'exquisite embarrassment' of silence, those involved resorted to a punch. In doing so they were true to their novel art form, one that has always been drawn to violence because of its own inherent violence – its desire to smack the viewer in the eye.

Naturally, there may be less metaphysical reasons for the choice of subject. Men who hope to sell the virtues of a device for the depiction of motion are not likely to choose a tea party as its test card. Boasting about his progress with a new cinema process, Thomas Edison declared that he had 'already perfected the invention so far as to be able to picture a prize-fight – the two men, the ring, the intensely interested faces of those surrounding it – and you can hear the blows'.* Edison's genius, along with all that proverbial perspiration, consisted of his ability to exploit his ideas commercially, and the subject matter he chooses here demonstrates his entrepreneurial acuity. He knew that some of the cinema's first box-office hits were straightforward recordings of real bouts – films such as *The Great Corbett Fight* of 1897, a match between James J. Corbett and Bob Fitzsimmons, which was filmed in Enoch Rector's Veriscope in a special arena constructed for the occasion. That film was 90 minutes long and received with rapt attention by audiences, something that seems inconceivable now, when the fascination of watching the few remaining fragments palls after only a few minutes (and is, in any case, artificially boosted by a sense of history). But the discrepancy serves to register the intense novelty of both subject and medium. To watch moving figures was enchantment enough; to see a prize fight – that forbidden, disreputable attraction – was additional bliss. The fight between Jeffries and Sharkey at Coney Island in 1899 was another huge success, with no fewer than four cameras being used to capture the action – one filming, one being focused, another being reloaded and another in reserve.

*Edison has some claim to have invented 'pay-per-view', since his later boxing films required the viewer to deliver another ten cents before they could see the following round.

And it isn't difficult to see why the boxing ring should prove so amenable to the needs of the new entertainment, well before its unshakeable addiction to narrative had set in. Technical, commercial and artistic motives all combine to render the nuptials all but inevitable. The boxing ring was a fixed arena suitable for the inflexible focusing of early cameras (it was not dissimilar in shape and size, in fact, to the crude theatrical stages on which the first dramas were filmed). What's more, boxing also offered an obvious model of entrepreneurship for an industry with no established conception of exactly what its product was. Boxing already knew about the creation of thrilling spectacle for a mass (often illiterate) audience: it knew how to use identifiable stars to draw a crowd. Above all, the boxing match supplied a ready-made drama, market-tested with the precise audience the producers hoped to exploit. Edison's little touch of descriptive colour – his portrayal of 'the intensely interested faces' – is actually a subtle perfume of profit insinuated into the middle of his sales pitch. That rapt audience conjured by Edison will hopefully be reflected by another one in the dark of the projection hall.

The association lasts for some time. David O. Selznick's very first film as a producer was *Will He Conquer Dempsey?*, a two-reeler made in 1922 which cannily exploited the fact that the American public knew nothing about Jack Dempsey's forthcoming opponent for an important fight, an Argentinian boxer called Luis Angel Firpo. The film was made in a single day for the cost of $2,059.71, and it is probable that Tex Rickard, Dempsey's promoter, helped to fund it – after all, a large gate depended on a widespread assumption of a close fight, an expectation that needed careful grooming. In its combination of ballyhoo, violent drama and guaranteed resolution, the sport of boxing could hardly be improved upon as an armature for the new entertainment. The physical combat of two people, with its inherent fluctuations of fortune and its natural rhythm of suspense and resolution, had always been one of the great elemental story-lines, and Hollywood (as well as other national cinemas) took it up eagerly. The boxing film has been a regular attraction, whether it's in the form of pugilistic biopics (*Gentleman Jim, The Great John L., Somebody up There Likes Me, The Great White Hope, Raging Bull*) or fictional accounts of the sport (*The Square Ring, The Square Jungle, Kid Galahad, The Champ, The Crowd Roars, The Set-Up, Golden Boy, The Good Die Young* and *Rocky*, to name only a selection).

The kinship of subject and medium has long been explicit in the genre: 'Everyone wants to be a champion, don't they?' asks the innocent bellhop turned prize-fighter in Michael Curtiz's *Kid Galahad* (1937). 'Even I wanted to be one once,' Bette Davis answers him. 'I was going to panic New York with dance and song.' Her abandoned expectations precisely mirror his rising ones, but what really binds the two is not just the kinship of boxing and showbiz but the essentially American recognition of the *innocence* of ambition, a repeated element in the guileless boxing films of the thirties and forties and a piece of wishful thinking that has still not lost its power. There is, naturally enough, a Freudian explanation for the genre's repeated use of a hero who appears naïve or 'dumb' in relation to the world in which he finds himself. In *The Uses of Enchantment*, Bruno Bettelheim notes:

> When the hero of a fairy tale is the youngest child, or is specifically called 'the dummy' or 'Simpleton' at the start of the story, this is the fairy tale's rendering of the original debilitated state of the ego as it begins its struggle to cope with the inner world of drives, and with the difficult problems the outer world presents.

This will go some way as an account of the fixed satisfactions of the early boxing films, which almost invariably include the exposure of a naïve hero to a world of darker appetites, but it does not serve to explain why it is that films take so much care to ensure that the initial simplicity remains intact. The joy of those early Hollywood fairy-tales is that the ego remains assertively, heroically 'debilitated', in Bettelheim's term. In *Kid*

Galahad the character teased for his bucolic name at the beginning – he is called Geesenberry and nicknamed Gooseberry by Edward G. Robinson's promoter – survives his transformation to medieval knight to achieve his hopes: the gal of his dreams and a farm to call his own. His ambition is acceptable because it is an ambition to have no ambition. The purse, corrupt as it might be, is ultimately purified by the use to which it is put. And though boxing films very rapidly become a genre of disenchantment, it is notable that those inside the ropes – the artistes, as it were – continue to be depicted as innocent of duplicity or ill at ease with its requirements. 'Tankers' – that is, boxers prepared to take a dive – frequently renege on their deals at the last moment, stung by sudden resurgence of conscience. Even when they comply, they display a grief at their fall that is inexplicable to those around them. This virtue does not have to be intelligent. The lumbering innocence of the duped boxer in *The Harder They Fall* is conveyed with beautiful economy by having him bump into a light-fitting on his first entrance, a detail that emphasizes both his size and his slow-witted vulnerability. But for all his obtuseness – the truth about his fixed 'victories' literally has to be punched into him before he will accept it – he remains the picture's conscience, a pole of honesty that guides those who have lost their moral direction.

Here, too, the kinship between boxing and cinema is at work, though in a more sophisticated form. The metaphor now works to identify conflicts of interest within these respective forms of entertainment, and it is hardly surprising that the creative talent of cinema, self-consciously at odds with the corrupting interferences of money-men and studio bosses, should incorporate into their pictures an implicit celebration of the moral superiority of the artist. Indeed, the equation between boxing and entertainment is almost never to the latter's credit, becoming, in later works, an established code for the corruption and fraudulence of the sport – in particular the sense that a ceremony of truth has been demeaned. In contradiction of the old song, there are many businesses like show business, but it's worse for them

that they are. In many films, the final showdown or climactic
fight represents the moment when compromise is rejected. The
exhilaration of those scenes is partly powered by the frustration
of those who created them, their clear identification with talent
subjected to improper discipline.

In *The Harder They Fall* (1956), Rod Steiger, the crooked
promoter who finagles a gentle Argentinian giant, El Toro, into
a championship contender, attempts to persuade a journalist
down on his luck (Humphrey Bogart, in his last screen
appearance) to collaborate in the creation of a fake contender:
'Listen to me, Lewis, you've got your sights all screwed up,' he
says. 'The fight game today is like show business. There's no
real fighters any more. The best showman becomes the champ.'
Although *The Harder They Fall* is a consistently bleak account
of the boxing game (it precedes *Sweet Smell of Success* by just
one year, a film with which it shares a marked similarity of
moral tone), it cannot bring itself to abandon the old satisfactions entirely: at the conclusion of the film Bogart restores El
Toro to his Argentinian mother and returns to his typewriter,
punching out the first sentence of an exposé of the underhand
plot we have just followed. Unfortunately our education in the
lengths to which greedy men will go to protect their investments
has been far too efficient to allow this to soothe us. The champion may be on his feet again, may even have knocked his
opponent Steiger on to the back foot, but you fear that the only
column likely to figure in Bogart's future will be made of concrete and supporting a freeway.

Much later – when the fashion for disenchantment had run
its course – Hollywood was to attempt to repudiate the cynical
analogy between showbiz and boxing in a film that reasserted
the fabulous innocence of the genre, but which in the long run
only confirmed the truth of Steiger's remark. *Rocky* was a film
that also temporarily revived Hollywood's cyclical vogue for
contes moraux in the form of pugilistic combat. (The vogue
culminated in one of the most complex of all boxing pictures,
Raging Bull, it being one of the industry's routine miracles that

the transitory may beget the enduring, even if only by changing the commercial climate. It's possible to wonder whether Scorsese would have found it as easy to make *Raging Bull* without the example of a box-office hit just a few years before and whether he was provoked by the casual religiosity of Stallone's fairy-tale. *Rocky* begins with a close-up of Christ and pulls back to reveal that we are in the Resurrection Athletic Club – an unimprovable name for a Hollywood gym.)

In *Rocky* (1976), the rough talent of the hero – dumb but tender – is opposed to the sophisticated commercial calculations of the champion Apollo Creed. Indeed, it is only Creed's sense for an exploitable story-line that brings the two men together in the first place, Rocky Balboa being a down-and-out southpaw who has been reduced to enforcing for loan sharks. He is emphatically not a contender. Faced with cancelling an important bout due to the lack of a reputable opponent, Creed comes up with a radical idea: 'This is the land of opportunity, right? So Apollo Creed on July 4th gives a local underdog fighter an opportunity.' Creed might almost be pitching a screenplay here – one that combines cynical exploitation of the great patriotic myths with the elemental tension of a scheduled combat (deferred but ineluctable violence being one of cinema's prime movers). He knows this fiction will sell tickets to the bout and, as it proved in 1976, it was also capable of selling surprising numbers of tickets to *Rocky*, one of the year's unexpected hits. It is a mark of Rocky's purity that he believes the fiction wholeheartedly. He is, despite his reduced circumstances, another avatar of the knightly contestant protected by his virtue. Immediately after the low-grade bout that introduces the film he is seen crooning at kittens in a pet-shop window and it is established, with slightly panicky haste, that he is a very bad enforcer, reluctant to break thumbs as his career requires. 'American history proves that everyone has a chance to win,' the underdog tells a press conference with unironic stolidity. As the climactic bout proceeds and Rocky endures his terrible beating, Creed's anxious corner-man whispers in the champion's ear: 'He doesn't know it's a damn show. He thinks it's a damn fight.'

One of the retrospective fascinations of *Rocky*, indeed, is the way in which its own production history and its narrative line become almost inextricable. The film ambitions of its previously unknown star and screenwriter are transferred into the fiction with undisguised directness, Stallone even giving to his character the same sobriquet – the Italian Stallion – under which he had performed in soft-porn films, the cinema's equivalent of the bottom-of-the-bill fights by which Rocky scrapes a living. And when the film triumphed (it won three Academy Awards), it did for Stallone's career what Creed's huckstering story-line had done for Rocky's. It doesn't even seem particularly ironic that the ingenuous charm of the first movie should have been corrupted by success, with increasingly bloated and preposterous sequels; that is merely another element in the complete congruence of life and art. 'Why do you want to fight?' asks Rocky's shy girlfriend. 'Because I cain't sing or dance,' he replies, reversing Bette Davis's analogy nearly forty years on. Now, it seems, boxing is showbiz for the tone deaf.

It might be objected here that boxing isn't punching – that this account of the cinematic appeal of pugilism isn't simply transferable to the vastly larger number of fights that take place outside the ring. That is true, of course. There are many other modulations of hand-to-hand combat in cinema, many other arenas that offer a similar sense of constriction and world-excluding focus – the dusty main street, the pool hall, the card table and the courtroom (what is *The Verdict*, in which Paul Newman's alcoholic lawyer returns to win one last hopeless case, but a classic prize-fighter's comeback?). But boxing feeds into mainstream cinema in a way that is difficult for other skills of competitive supremacy.

We needn't establish a simple line of heredity here. Fist-fighting doesn't engender cinema, even if it's possible to argue that it assisted at the birth; both spectacles are manifestations of older instincts. But within the art form, the fist-fight can claim a genuine precedence – the first punch is thrown before the first shot is fired or the first sword unsheathed – and it exerts a lasting influence. It offers weapons that are never anachronistic, always at hand. They are also weapons that can be deployed in almost any sphere – even that of the war film or the gangster movie, where a far more powerful armoury is usually available – and will increasingly be employed as the century discards its innocence. Liberated from the ring, where its functional power is narrowly defined (a punch is for winning) and its communicative power virtually non-existent, the punch rapidly ascends to the status of a cinematic *expression*. I use this word less for its precision than for its fruitful ambiguities, which helpfully encompass some of the contradictions of cinematic meaning, in particular the paradox that novelty and freshness can be created through the use of stock forms. 'Expression' will carry three slightly different concepts, all of which may be present in a screen punch. It has, first of all, the sense of a familiar phrase or cliché, the sort of utterance that is owned in common by all speakers of a language (as in 'a well-known expression'). Second, it retains the possibility of a specific and private communication ('it was a clear expression of his intentions'). Last of all, it can also suggest the sense of a hidden essence pressed out into the light, the idea of something squeezed from its containing medium, as oil is pressed from a nut.

It isn't part of the ambitions of this book to add to the glut of theoretical language that stifles much writing about cinema, one of the convictions on which it rests being that any attempt to codify cinematic meaning, or to construct some durable typebox into whose compartments its pleasures can be graded and sorted, is doomed to failure. But the word 'expression' is useful, I think, to describe those elements of popular cinema in which repetition and invention may combine (other examples of the cinematic expression might be: the kiss, the chase, the shootout – in other words, most of the sacramental rites of narrative). And one theoretical curiosity needs noting here about the punch. It is a significant exception to the cinema's broad rule that the real world is ransacked for meaningful objects – which still retain the full force of their 'objectness'. Onscreen, the rose that (perhaps) represents virginity is also likely to be a real rose, accounted for in the production budget, susceptible to the heat of the lights, doomed to wilt when the shooting is done. But the punch, however grimly realistic (and grimness and realism are always assumed to be proportionately related in this century) is virtually never the real thing. Actors, to paraphrase E.M. Forster, must never connect. Of course, something similar is true of many things that appear onscreen: a longing look, an angry argument, a death-defying fall. But in its combination of physical solidity and emotional intangibility the punch occupies an unusual position. If it is a stunt then it is one that must flow from the psychological content of the scene surrounding it – we should be able to say whether it was an angry or frustrated punch, a justified or unjustified one. Such an emotional qualification would be absurd in the case of a fall or a car crash, which have a more purely mechanical nature. At the same time, the punch's plausibility onscreen is not something that is particularly subject to the talent of the actor. True, some actors are better at throwing a punch than others – Howard Hawks complained that he hurt his arm teaching Montgomery Clift to punch in *Red River*. But the skill was teachable in a way that pure acting isn't, and necessarily so. When directors are struggling to extract emotion from the incompetent, the classic solution has always been provocation rather than education – a calculated abuse that results in genuine tears or genuine anger, which can then be captured and aimed in a different direction by the editing. But similar methods can hardly be used for the punch, for safety's sake if nothing else.

The point is made by an anecdote recounted by Errol Flynn in his autobiography. While making *Gentleman Jim*, the star had real difficulties during his scenes with Jack Loper, a genuine heavyweight who was not always able to forget his boxing instincts. Loper repeatedly hit Flynn for real in their scenes together until the exasperated actor finally threatened to retaliate with a bottle. Loper at once became next to useless, his cautious swings giving the scene an undesirable comedy. In order to stimulate his aggression once more, Flynn claims to have kicked him in the testicles – at which point he was instantly knocked cold by the ex-fighter. One doesn't have to swallow this story whole, Hollywood memoirs being almost as creative with the facts as the movies themselves. Indeed, *Gentleman Jim* is distinguished by some singularly unconvincing fight scenes in which both participants are clearly flailing at each other's chests (a common flaw in the poorer boxing pictures). But even so, the story conveys a simple truth about the distinction between reality and realism, the latter being cinema's entirely synthetic distillation of the former. A failure to distinguish between the two indicates either that the actor is punch-drunk (as seems to have been the case with Loper) or malicious. Flynn also claimed to have had trouble with Bette Davis during the filming of *The Private Lives of Elizabeth and Essex*, which includes a scene in which the Queen slaps her favourite. Davis's hands were freighted with costume jewellery – a kind of regal knuckleduster – and she withheld nothing in her rehearsal for the shot. When Flynn protested she made a defensive appeal to verisimilitude: 'I knew you were going to complain. I can't do it any other way! If I have to pull punches I can't do this!' She was persuaded of cinema's considerable powers of suggestion after Flynn promised her that he would return any further blow ounce for ounce.

The punch then might be taken as a classic instance of cinema's long negotiation between the real and artificial, a moment when Lumière and Méliès form some kind of *rapprochement*. Historically, though, this is a relationship in which the Lumière brothers have slowly gained the ascendancy – if we are to take their name as representative of a reverence for the depiction of the world as it really is. The punch in cinema is always a trick of the light but it matures towards its own carefully constructed authenticity, in particular through an

increasingly scrupulous inclusion of its consequences, which
comes to be seen as a moral obligation – not simply an increase
in verisimilitude. And while the result might sometimes be ugly
onscreen it meets a grander aesthetic programme: the pious
appreciation of the virtues of clear sight.

Silent cinema always had a problem with the punch because
of the absence of sound. Although the orchestra drummer could
add a percussive sting or a burlesque clash of the symbols as
fist (or pie) struck face, the result was almost bound to be
vaudevillian in its tone. Many fights in early cinema were visibly
lacklustre and the solution was either to film the real thing and
live with the physical consequences – as was done in *The
Spoilers* – or to 'pull' the punch as it connected, a fine muscular
judgement that invariably leaves its mark on the final gesture
(if not on the face of the actor's opposite number). For one
thing, these punches seem to have no moment; they stop sharply
on the face, betraying their lack of weight. For another, as
Buster Keaton remarked in a note on custard-pie technique, it
is a very disciplined actor indeed who can prevent a flinch from
announcing the imminent blow. When Humphrey Bogart slaps
Walter Brennan in *To Have and Have Not*, Brennan winces as
Bogart's arm begins its rise, an involuntary spasm that would
make sense if the two men had a long history of violence but
that effectively contradicts the script's assertion that this is the
first blow exchanged between them. Fortunately, this betraying
flaw is effectively invisible unless you use a stop-frame video to
catch it, but it illustrates Keaton's point all the same.

The classic Hollywood screen punch, in which the fist could
be carried past its point of impact by the impetus of the blow,
was the collaborative invention of John Wayne and Yakima
Canutt, the celebrated stuntman with whom Wayne worked on
innumerable cheap B-Westerns (as well as some durable classics,
such as *Stagecoach*). 'It wasn't that they were great inventive
geniuses,' recalled a colleague, 'it was pure expediency. They
raced through film after film with such speed that if they'd
carried on the old system of screen fighting – where actors

actually hit each other's shoulders – they'd have been eternally black and blue.' But the result of Wayne and Canutt's innovation – a full-bodied punch that could leave a safety margin between fist and chin provided the camera angle was right – was categorically not an increase in reality, as Wayne noted himself:

> A film fight is the opposite of a real fight because the camera has to see everything. You have to reach way back and sock out and make a big show. In a real fight you hit short and close. You don't get time to pull your punches back so far.

This offers us Duke as a semiotician identifying in his laconic drawl what it would have taken a professional academic many more words to say less clearly – the screen punch is always a sign of a punch, semaphored through the arms and shoulders of the actors.*

And if the punch clearly is a sign, it is also one that is almost diagramatically revealing about the way in which film can assemble emotional reality for its viewers. The meaning of a punch does not lie simply in the way it is thrown, just as the meaning of a glance or a line of dialogue is unlikely to reside solely within that one shot (a truth famously demonstrated by Lev Kuleshov's montage experiment, in which three identical shots of an actor's expressionless face were intercut with a plate of soup, a woman in a coffin and a little girl – and accordingly registered as hunger, grief and tender affection by the audience). The punch thrown by John Wayne in *Rio Bravo* is, some local details aside, effectively indistinguishable from that thrown by Bob Hope in *The Paleface*. What separates the two is what

---

*And as a sign, the punch has always offered the rhetorical effect of synecdoche. 'You can have a small army of people charging across the screen, and it won't matter much to the audience. But if you show the details of the action, like guns going off, individual men fighting or a fist hitting someone in the eye, then you will have more feeling of action than if all the extras in Hollywood are running about,' said B. Reeves Eason, a famous second-unit director whose credits include the chariot race in *Ben-Hur* and the burning of Atlanta in *Gone with the Wind*.

happens next: blood and unconsciousness in the case of the first, indifference and comically smarting knuckles in the second.

In other words, the punch is always a reaction shot or it is nothing. The recoil of an opponent's head measures the force of the blow, and this is true even on the occasions when a director frames a fight in middle or long shot, relying on the soundtrack for punctuation rather than an edit. (The words 'punch' and 'punctuate' share a distant ancestor, so we shouldn't be too surprised that the former serves to emphasize the latter in so many films.) Unless the victim's body or head registers the non-existent impact, it is unlikely to strike the audience with any force. More often than not, though, cutting is employed, as if to reinforce the image of the blow with an impact on the very retina of the viewer. And this has a connection with the essentially assaultive nature of the film cut itself. Repudiating Dziga Vertov's proselytization of the camera's worth as a tool of objective documentation, Eisenstein scorned the idea of 'kino-eye', far too passive and accepting an organ for his taste. 'I don't believe in kino-eye,' he declared. 'I believe in kino-fist.' He disagreed with Vsevolod Pudovkin, too, arguing that the meaning of an edit (or 'montage', in his terms) arose not from the linking of two ideas but from the collision of ideas they represented. Conflict wasn't just a subject matter for cinema; it was a method.

Eisenstein had political reasons for the aggression of his language here, but you don't need a commitment to Hegelian dialectic or revolutionary struggle to generate tough talk in directors. The vocabulary of cinematic effect has always leant towards attack rather than seduction – to knocking their eyes out, stunning an audience, rocking them back in their seats, smacking them in the face. To some degree this is an inherited language – ideas of impact in the arts long preceding the invention of cinema – but it is taken up with particular zeal by the medium, because it speaks so directly to the kinetic possibilities of the screen, the way in which it can inflict a violent alteration of vision on an audience. Unconsciousness is never part of the deal, naturally, but a kind of stunned submission may be. And the sense that the viewer is momentarily disorientated by such devices isn't just a metaphorical fancy. The film editor Donn Cambern tells the following story:

> In *Hooper* we had a wonderful bar fight where one character is dressed as a Roman gladiator, with breastplates, a sword at one side and a toga. He draws back his fist in a wide shot and the cut happens as he swings, then we cut to another angle because that's where the hit is best as far as the person who gets hit and what happens to him afterwards. But on the cut the character doesn't have his breastplates! In the frame before the cut he's in full regalia; in the frame right after, he's not. I've never heard anyone mention that they saw that, and it's flat in front of your face.*

Even as amiable a director as Jean Renoir could be seduced by the way in which editing allowed him to jar the sensibilities of his audience. 'Rapid cutting fascinated me,' he recalled in his autobiography *My Life and My Films*. 'Some of the shots in *La Fille de l'Eau* consisted of no more than five frames. The dazed audience feels as though it has been hit in the eye.' Renoir was later to outgrow such effects, repudiating them in favour of uncut sequences – the impact of which might pass by the less alert viewer, but the temptation is a perpetual one for directors. The punch is a place where the aggressive appetites of the director find an alibi in the very matter he or she is presenting, so it has quite naturally become associated with 'in your face' editing and direction.

It's a nice irony, in this respect, that the only use of the word 'punch' in the Motion Picture Production Code of 1930 (the document by which the moral health of Hollywood was supposedly to be regulated) occurs in a note explaining the rules about costume: 'Nudity or semi-nudity used simply to put a "punch"

---

* First Cut: Conversations with Film Editors, Gabriella Oldham, University of California Press, 1992.

in a picture comes under the head of immoral actions.' The Production Code contains no specific inhibitions on fight scenes, although it does decree that brutal killings are not to be presented in detail and warns, under the heading of Repellent Subjects, that 'third degree methods' must be 'treated within the limits of good taste'. In an age more sensitive about physical violence, this absence of anxiety seems to need explanation, and there is a relatively simple one at hand. Although some producers had expressed unease about the early association of cinema and boxing – a morally disreputable sport that, it was thought, might drive away 'respectable' audiences – the punch and the fight are very quickly rehabilitated as moral actions, used to represent the triumph of good over evil (through the manly agency of the fist) or as a manifestation of moral determination.

There are bullies who resort to the fist, naturally (particularly in early comedies), but there is no inhibition about returning violence with violence. Fights are manifestly part of early cinema's code of purity not of degeneracy, and the absence of concern in the Production Code is proof of that – a dog that doesn't bark because it is not remotely alarmed. When the Code seeks an example for a 'wrong entertainment', the kind that might lower 'the whole living conditions and moral ideals of a race', it offers 'cockfighting, bullfighting, bearbaiting etc.', neglecting the existence of a more proximate human equivalent which had been the subject of moral queasiness for years (boxing was illegal in many states, a circumstance that only whetted the appetite for early boxing films). 'Note too,' the Code continued, 'the effect on ancient nations of gladiatorial combats' – a historic aside that implies that modern nations might be equally at risk but seems to take it for granted that they haven't already created a substitute for the bloody satisfactions of the Circus. Using a punch to put 'punch' into a picture seems to have been acceptable from the beginning.

But if the punch allows the cinema's instincts of assault to be revealed with unusual candour, it is also a gesture capable of rich ambiguities. It is striking (even the critical vocabulary acknowledges the force of a blow) to see what a range of feeling can be extracted from this single narrative component, just one of the building blocks on which genre cinema draws for its affective structure. Even in the work of a single director, the elementary collision of fist and face can reflect odd and unfamiliar lights. Howard Hawks, a great proponent of the punch both in front of and behind the camera, found ways to introduce a complexity of feeling into what had become a ritual gesture of action cinema. He converted its simple noise of clashing antlers into a subtle, insinuating dialogue.

One of the more intriguing examples can be found in *The Big Sky*, his 1952 film about a fur-trading expedition up the Missouri River. Like many Hawks films, it is much taken up with the grounds of male companionship and it begins with an encounter of compelling asymmetry. Travelling alone through the woods, Kirk Douglas is saved from a snake by Dewey Martin, but, as he approaches to thank him for his intervention, Martin punches him without warning, a swift uppercut that sends Douglas sprawling backwards. His response to this apparently unprovoked assault is surprisingly mild – the obvious question ('What'cha do that fer?'), followed by a wry stroke of his unmarked chin and an example of the actor's trademark predatory leer. It is the gesture of a man responding to a stolen intimacy rather than a humiliating challenge. Douglas rises slowly with an ambiguous line of complaint: 'I don't like to be hit, especially when I ain't looking for it.' He is punched to the ground again, a repetition that still doesn't ignite his anger. And then, his notional affront having been allayed, Martin refuses to fight on, on the grounds that Douglas has sprained his ankle. The convention of the fair fight is invoked by a man who has just signally betrayed it. That the fight remains unresolved is understood by both men, and the lack of satisfactory reciprocity is what binds them together. 'I don't wanna lose you,' says Douglas, as they travel on together. 'You won't,' Martin assures him, a sardonic pledge of fidelity based on the desire to complete the fight.*

This knuckled communion, it's worth noting, is not simply one of those attitudes that exist only onscreen. It had a real equivalent in Hawks's own male friendships, which appear to have been bracing, to say the least. Asked once why two of his films contained scenes in which a man has a dislocated finger pulled back into position by a friend, Hawks replied by questioning his interviewer: 'You ever hit anybody hard? Your finger goes out of joint, and somebody takes it and pulls it back into joint. I hit Hemingway and I broke the whole back of my hand. I wish it *had* just gone out of joint.' 'Why did you hit Hemingway?' asked the interviewer, assuming there must have been some grounds for the punch. 'He just said, "Can you hit?" I broke my whole hand. He laughed like hell, and he sat up all night making a splint out of a tomato can so that I could go shooting with him the next morning.'

At the very end of *The Big Sky*, as the two men prepare to part, the debt of unmatched blows surfaces again. Douglas hands Martin an extra bag of lead shot, and as he does so he adds an allusion to the fact that Martin has previously used this object to add weight to his punches: 'There's times in the past days I wanted to give it to you different,' he says. 'Still do it,' replies Martin, with a note of invitation in his voice. 'There'll be time for that next year when I come back,' says Douglas, his caricature knife-slash smile gleaming again. The two words that you can incontrovertibly apply to these exchanges are 'flirtatious' and 'suggestive'; it is a seductive sword dance that thrills because it treads so close to the cutting edge of the men's feelings for each other. The punch here is a form of assay, a

---

*This isn't the only instance of encounters that break the rule that a punch is always returned by the hero. In *The Man Who Shot Liberty Valance*, John Wayne accepts a punch from James Stewart without returning it, after he has humiliated Stewart. The scene is partly evidence of Stewart's lack of strength but it also registers Wayne's sense of a debt paid off. To punch back would make him a bully, and that is not his role here.

way of testing the mettle of a man, but also a means of reaching out to him.

Such scenes are liable to provoke smirks these days by their apparently unwitting revelation of desire, the canonical case being the admiring exchange in *Red River* between Montgomery Clift and John Ireland, when the two young men compare their handguns. It is no longer possible to screen this sequence (which is manifestly about boyishness, rather than subterranean yearnings) without knowing laughter from a cinema audience, but it is worth asking what precisely the laughter knows, and whether the object of its scorn might be a forgotten sophistication rather than a loss of innocence. Hawks's films remind us that it is possible for male relationships to display a non-sexual eroticism – a kind of amorous play that has no thought of consummation. If there is a sublimation here, it is the sublimation not of homosexuality but of affection, which has to find expression through one of the few forms of physical contact permitted between action heroes (though a kind of mischievous joke about Clift's sexuality can't be entirely ruled out).

Now that the policemen of sexual politics have been retrained, scenes such as the opening of *The Big Sky* can easily be framed as symptomatic of gender disorder – a kind of psychopathic repression of feeling. But that would be far too simplistic a dismissal of their muscular language. The punch, in Hawks, is rarely just an angry spasm of frustrated or denied feeling; it is a communication of some exactitude about what men can offer to each other. In *Red River*, for example, the first blow struck by John Wayne is a therapeutic slap, the classic Hollywood cure for hysteria, and it is important that his hand remains open because the recipient of this rough medicine is just a child, the young Matthew Garth still in shock after witnessing the massacre of his family in the wagon train. The second blow, also open-handed, is pedagogical and more dubious in its effect on an audience. 'Never trust a stranger,' growls Wayne, delivering the first lesson in his arid survivalist morality (a morality that the film persistently questions without ever quite disavowing – after all, it is down to Wayne's willing-ness to notch the empty landscape with graves that there are any cattle to drive at all).

The slap is a mark of unequal fighting weight, a brutality offered by senior to junior. (Or in many films from male to female. When a man does punch a woman in the classical Hollywood film, as Cary Grant punches Ingrid Bergman in *Notorious*, the sight is screened from us by his broad back, a recognition that in 1946 this was still too much to be shown explicitly.) The slap is justified, within the moral structures of *Red River*, as an accompaniment to the conferring of wisdom. And in the final showdown, when Wayne pushes aside the longhorn cattle to confront Montgomery Clift for his insurrection on the trail, it is crucial that it is a slap and not a punch that he first metes out after failing to provoke Clift into drawing his gun – it is still the punishment for a child not a man.

In an earlier version of the script Wayne was to have fought Clift knowing that he had a bullet wound in the shoulder. 'Do you think I'd have fought him with fists if he hadn't?' Wayne says. 'He'd have killed me. Don't forget, I taught him how to fight.' But that explicit recognition of what is involved here – a succession of power – would have left matters unresolved. In the final version, matters are no less clear but involve more free will on both sides (a bullet in the shoulder being a stark disincentive to give it your best shot). Clift makes no attempt to return the first slap, a kind of dumb insolence that makes it plain he no longer recognizes the validity of Wayne's corrective violence. The next blow is a punch, and in the simple clenching of his fingers Wayne effectively acknowledges Clift's transition to manhood, a covenant of equal standing which is sealed when Clift responds with a punch of his own and the men's feud can end in an honourable discharge of feeling. While Clift's hands hang by his side, Wayne's humiliation will remain unsalved, however brutal the beating he inflicts. 'You ain't worth fighting' has always been one of the Western's most stinging insults. It is not Wayne's punch that settles the debt but Clift's, at once acknowledging his 'father's' authority and marking its termination.

This apparent paradox – the blow that heals – is hardly unique to *Red River*. Indeed, it is one of the fixed tropes of the punch in Hollywood movies. In John Ford's *The Searchers* there is a good example of a scene that will surely flicker in anyone's mental repertory cinema – the long, scuffling punch-up that takes the inimical energies of two men and converts them into an exhausted, bleeding fraternity. Martin has returned to find that his long-suffering sweetheart is about to marry Charlie, a comically genial hick who has the sole romantic virtue of guaranteed presence. The scene that follows is played for low comedy, the principal joke being the distinction between the etiquette with which the duel is arranged ('Spit over that piece of firewood,' says Charlie, inviting Martin to commence hostilities formally) and the instant abandonment of rules. 'Fight fair, no biting or gouging,' says one of the bystanders, a line for which the visual full stop is a boot to the chin.

The fight that follows is a compendium of low blows, a contained abandonment of civilization eagerly watched by those who might be expected to speak for its virtues – the preacher, the Texas Ranger and the women who have been shooed away inside but crowd to the windows to gawp. Religion, law and domestic virtue all succumb to the excitement. This is a social ceremony and it ends, as it must, with an exhausted parity and words of peace: 'Sorry I bit yer ear, Marty.' 'Oh, it don't hurt none.' Of course it don't hurt none, because punches never do in this species of fight. Faces remain unmarked – but for a discreet trickle of blood which acts as a mere logo for healable injury.

Four years earlier Ford had delivered an even more elaborate version of this scene in *The Quiet Man*, a romantic comedy that steadily works its way towards just such a brawl. *The Quiet Man* is a great film only if one utters the phrase in tones of condescending affection. Its pleasures for a modern audience, like those of many period films, involve our reconstructing what it must have been like to take the work at face value, and then savouring the innocence of that response. But it isn't without its darker ambiguities – the rambling picaresque fight that resolves the film (ending Wayne's strained pacifism and resolving the issue of Maureen O'Hara's dowry) follows a long preamble, in which Wayne drags his hot-tempered wife across the countryside to witness the confrontation. His earlier refusal to fight is inexplicable to her (or at least explicable only by cowardice) but not to us; we have seen the mental flashback that reveals how Wayne killed an opponent during his boxing career, a tragedy that led to his renunciation of the punch.

The sequence with O'Hara is fraught with repressed violence (although Wayne limits himself to a brutal and humiliating disregard for O'Hara's equilibrium, so that she half runs and is half dragged after him) and the sense of relief that arrives when he finally punches Danaher is only partly to do with their long-deferred collision. Wayne's frustration, which is sexual too, has found an acceptable outlet. That notional trauma, incidentally, does not affect the weight of Wayne's punches at all, having only a structural purpose in the film – that of postponement – rather than a psychological one. And here, too, we find that it is the breaking of regulation that is at the heart of our pleasure. 'Marquess of Queensbury rules!' shouts one of the excited bystanders, a shout taken up by others and finally repeated by Wayne in sardonic bemusement. As he completes the final syllable he is kicked in the face by his opponent, an almost identical moment to that in *The Searchers*. And as in *The Searchers*, the conclusion is universal amity (delayed here by a break for a pint of porter and the observance of several of Hollywood's own Queensbury rules: that at least one participant in a film brawl shall be knocked into a river or water-trough; that if a man is down the offer of a hand by his opponent shall be taken as permission to resume hostilities without warning; that opponents will take turns to be on the receiving end; that any protagonist who turns away as if to cede the fight will then whirl round unexpectedly and deliver a mighty hook to his opponent's jaw).*

It would be difficult to mount a very convincing account of these as morally subtle scenes – they are knockabout and predictable knockabout at that. But while it is conventional now to think of this kind of consequence-free violence as a mark of Hollywood's shallow duplicity – a notably false instruction in the ways of the world – it is easy to be myopic about what else such scenes can offer us. There is a different way of stating the conclusion to which they come, which would see it not as a consoling lie about violent disorder but as a kind of assertion: that enmity can be overcome, that anger may not end only in injury or death, that order can be restored. This is to present violence not as a therapy in itself – though it can look very much like that given the universal glee it provokes – but rather as a survivable breakdown. The strenuous assertion of rules emphasizes the chaos that follows but also reminds us that a code of behaviour exists against which the fights can be measured.†

There is something decidedly vintage about such scenes, though, because violence in the movies becomes less survivable as the decades pass. Indeed, the exact degree of damage done will often date a film as effectively as the cars in the street – more so, perhaps, given cinema's long-standing passion for time travel. And this is not just a mark of age but of an increasing uncertainty about the very depiction of violence. Lawrence

*The idea of applying 'rules' to events that are so conspicuously unregulated has proved durably fruitful. There is a notable scene in *Butch Cassidy and the Sundance Kid* in which Butch defeats an attempted coup by one of his gang members by insisting that they 'get the rules straight' before they begin their gladiatorial contest. 'What rules?' asks his puzzled opponent, at which point Butch boots him in the groin and says, 'No kicking.'

†Scorsese, who quotes the brawl from *The Searchers* in *Mean Streets*, certainly has a kind of fraternity in mind when he produces a contemporary equivalent of Ford's comic violence with the pool-hall fight, which begins with an almost formal breach of etiquette (the epithet 'mook', which no one understands but is deemed to qualify as grounds for combat) and ends with a curious absence of grievance.

Alloway notes, in his book *Violent America*, that 'we can index heroes by the amount of dirt they collect in fighting and running, by the number of their injuries and the length of time needed to heal'. Similarly, in his book *Westerns* Philip French argues:

> [T]he tone of fistfights is usually a key to a film's approach to violence. In the ... films of John Ford and his natural successor Andrew V. McLaglen, these fights are hardly ever taken seriously. They are usually conducted between comrades and friendly rivals.

He opposes these amicable brawls, orgies of traded blows that leave their participants curiously sated, with the harsher fights of Anthony Mann, bloody and relentless and occasionally even fatal. While one couldn't take issue with French's fine description of those bacchanals of damage, it's possible to question the assumption that their sense of jubilation simply equates to a lack of seriousness – if we are to take that as synonymous with the absence of significant content.* Still, it would be a little perverse to quibble over this, because I know what French means – and so would anyone with even the most meagre sense of the trajectory of mood that movies follow over this century. Pauline Kael, in an essay written in 1973, describes it with enviable assurance:

> The movies of the Thirties said that things would get better. The post-Second World War movies said that villainy would be punished and goodness would triumph; the decencies would be respected. But movies don't say that anymore; the

---

*It's worth pausing, incidentally, to reflect on how rare it is, outside circles of specialist knowledge, that a critic can confidently allude to a generalized convention in the way that French refers to these barroom brawls. It would be virtually impossible to do anything remotely similar with the novel, to summon a vivid, generalized picture of what a fight or a kiss might consist of on the page, even if one was to take genre fiction as the source. The closest analogies we can find are probably themes in visual art – Annunciations or still lifes – where the components of a scene and their arrangement can be broadly predicted. It is a fact that presses home to what a large degree the cinema audience 'knows the form'.

58

Vietnamization of American movies is nearly complete. Today, movies say that the system is corrupt, that the whole thing stinks, and they've been saying this steadily since the mid-Sixties.

The descent begins surprisingly late in her version, I think, given the long roster of fifties films that offer the astringent modern satisfaction of justified disgust. Billy Wilder's *Ace in the Hole*, a film in which a newly bereaved wife declines to kneel in prayer because it will ruin her new stockings, was released in 1951, long before Vietnam could have afflicted the national consciousness. But the curve is broadly accurate nonetheless. And the punch naturally shared the same gravitational movement towards a self-dramatizing pessimism.

It has been easy to associate this with external political causes, with the disenchantment learnt painfully in the world. It is as if the gap between the visions of Hollywood and knowledge of the post-war world grew too large to be sustained. The world would not move so cinema had to. It had to accommodate the regrettable disillusionment of its audience. But it's possible that the shift was accelerated by what began as a purely aesthetic programme, the increasing prestige of disillusionment in another sense – one in which the illusions are implicitly regarded not as cherishable but as a clouding of the vision. In 'The Ontology of the Photographic Image' (written in 1945), André Bazin argued approvingly that the cinema killed off by the arrival of sound – the cinema of gestural montage and expressionistic image – was not '*the* cinema' , as some mourners had declared, but something closer to a negotiated settlement, a mere holding position until technology caught up enough to add sound and complete the picture. What replaces silent cinema is not a corrupted form – now tainted by language – but a liberated one. Bazin writes:

> The aesthetic qualities of photography are to be sought in its power to lay bare the realities. It is not for me to separate off, in the complex fabric of the objective world, here a

reflection on a damp sidewalk, there the gesture of a child. Only the impassive lens, stripping its object of all those ways of seeing it, those piled up preconceptions, that spiritual dust and grime with which my eyes have covered it, is able to present it in all its virginal purity to my attention and consequently to my love.

Bazin chooses his examples carefully – the lyricism of the everyday (rain on the pavement) and the dependable charm of childhood – and then sets these desirable truths against the bleary vision that it is photography's duty to correct. The implication is that 'laying bare' and 'stripping' will remove a polluted veil from the world and open it up for our love.

In practice, though, the images this dream of purity generated were likely to be much harsher. We are given a clearer sight of what results in *The Evolution of the Language of Cinema* (written between 1950 and 1955), in which Bazin has this to say about Erich von Stroheim:

> In his films reality lays itself bare like a suspect confessing under the relentless examination of the commissioner of police. He has one simple rule for direction. Take a close look at the world, keep on doing so, and in the end it will lay bare for you all its cruelty and its ugliness.

'Laying bare' suddenly sounds a good deal less benevolent in its effects, a revelation not of the world's essential beauty but of the squalor that lay concealed behind that 'spiritual dust and grime'. And while one would hardly want to argue that a French theorist directed the course of post-war cinema, these passages are representative of a widespread prejudice of the second half of the century – that close inspection is, on the whole, more likely to lead to disillusion than to consolation. The association between scrutiny and detection, and the idea that interrogating the world closely will usually lead to the revelation of crime, becomes fixed. We know too much about false confessions these days for Bazin's analogy to be quite comfortable. There is the sense that the world could all too easily end up as the victim of a miscarriage of justice, convicted of crimes that it never actually committed. But that is not how it looked in the sixties and seventies, when 'unblinking vision' and 'sharp sight' are almost never associated with an acquittal, or with the discovery that the world is a kinder place than we had assumed. And it is hardly surprising that the cinematic punch would fall under suspicion in such a climate. If anything needed its accretions of myth and conceptual habit chipping away, then surely it was the way in which cinema had adapted the fight and the blow for its own purposes, neglecting the consequences of violence in favour of the familiar choreography of punch and recoil. Those directors who made their fight sequences more conspicuously bloody were not simply reflecting post-war dismay at the brutality of life; they were part of an aesthetic tendency, too.

The natural end point of this development is *Raging Bull* – a film in which cinema's long infatuation with boxing meets this aesthetic of purified (and purifying) vision. In her review of the film, Pauline Kael noted pertinently that '*Raging Bull* isn't a biographical film about a fighter's rise and fall; it's a biography of the genre of prizefight films.'* She is certainly right about its visual content. Scorsese takes the well-loved furniture of the genre – the numbered round cards, the fussing corner-men, the eager crowd – but he employs them as allusions to a carefully excluded sense of urgency. *Raging Bull* is almost unique among fight pictures for the fact that we care nothing about whether Jake La Motta wins or loses his bouts, and nothing in Scorsese's film is designed to arouse our allegiances. The montaged round cards, which in more conventional films had paced the agony for the viewer, have no instructive content but their sense of place. There are precedents, too, for the film's explicit depiction of the damage that can be done by a trained fighter. *The Set-Up*, a bleak and claustrophobic tragedy of failed ambitions, includes a scene in which a boxer's gum-shield drops

Taking It All In, Pauline Kael, Marion Boyars, 1995.

to the canvas, gleaming with bloody saliva. In *The Harder They Fall* you see the blood flowing, an unprotected fall to the canvas, the halo of sweat that a punch knocks free from a boxer's face. In *The Quiet Man*, a film Scorsese alludes to directly as a source, Wayne's memory of the fatal bout is accompanied by the pop of flashbulbs – a detail Scorsese turned into luminous slurred echoes of punches themselves. Even *Rocky* registered the damage inflicted by repeated blows, the way in which a man's face can be converted into a Francis Bacon portrait, flesh smeared into a cartoon of his own features.*

So what is radical about *Raging Bull* is not so much that the ring is seen as a realm of genuine violence for the first time, but that there is no respite outside the ropes and no sympathetic alibi for what we see. *Raging Bull* must also be one of the few fight pictures in which you feel a sense of relief when the bell rings to start the fighting – and not because a moment of resolution has finally arrived but because this violence at least has some explanation, has an end in sight. In the event, Scorsese withholds even that grim refuge (the consolation of the ring as a taming force, a place that will alchemically transform unacceptable rage into a means of achievement). When La Motta savagely beats an opponent his wife has praised as attractive, isolating his face as a target for viciously destructive punches, he effectively erases the ropes as a boundary that distinguishes the professional from the personal.

It might reasonably be objected that *Raging Bull* is too expressionistic in its fight sequences to fit this account of an aesthetic of clinical examination. But the fact that the boxing scenes are the occasions for displays of manipulative bravura – slow motion, stop-motion, freeze frame – actually leads us back to dispassionate clarity of observation. Such techniques are as much at home in a laboratory as in the art-house movie. Talking of his preparation for the film, Scorsese mentions *Kiss of Death*,

*It's not very surprising to discover that Bacon was actually a fan of the *Rocky* series.

a film he found fascinating for its look ('Twentieth Century Fox under the Italian Neo-Realist influence') and his account of visits to Madison Square Garden are victories of redirected vision – looking away from the magnetic spectacle in the ring to the tiny particulars that go unnoticed in the excitement: the bloodied sponge and the blood dripping from the rope. ('As the next bout was announced no one took any notice of it,' says Scorsese with the artist's unmistakable note of triumph at gleaning an overlooked detail from the world.)* In this respect, Scorsese's stylistic devices have less to do with emotional amplification than with an exactitude of perception. When we see the blood on that umbilical rope, burgeoning to a drop and then releasing with languid gravity, our attitude is closer to a reverence for the beauty of the thing than it is to any summoned empathy for the man who shed it. The title card that concludes the film finally unites an aesthetic morality with a religious one: 'I once was blind but now I see', a text from St Matthew's gospel which echoes Bazin's call for a cinema that will remove the scales from our eyes.

Such moments in *Raging Bull* alert us to an oddity in our casual vocabulary about cinematic violence. For years now the ready cliché for extreme brutality onscreen, brutality that includes aftermath in its composition, has been the phrase 'graphic violence'. There is no solecism here – as an intensifier, 'graphic' has a long history, with examples from the mid-seventeenth century of its use to mean 'vividly descriptive' or 'lifelike' – but its transference to screen violence since the war also involves an amnesia about its literal meaning, which has to do with drawing, the handmade creation of an image, with all the implications that has for a mediated vision of the word. What we see onscreen, when a halo of blood or brain-matter splashes the wall behind a gunshot victim or when a single hard punch shatters the nose of its recipient, is not 'graphic violence' in fact but 'photographic violence'. It is light that draws the

Scorsese on Scorsese, ed. Ian Christie, Faber, London, 1997.

picture and, even if special effects are required to achieve the end result, all the effort is bent on replicating the camera's unsparing attention to detail. 'Graphic violence', in truth, might more appropriately be applied to the films of Howard Hawks and his peers – those films in which the exchange of blows becomes another medium for the utterance of emotional truths. And in that sense, graphic violence has almost entirely disappeared from the screen, to be replaced either by a clinical realism (a vision often lauded or defended as 'uncompromising', as if anything else would be evidence of a blind eye turned) or a cheap gag. Photography congratulates itself on its rigour of vision when, more often than not, it transforms the depiction of violence into an aesthetic rather than a moral experience, while at the other extreme the cartoon punch-ups of the action movies abandon any attempt to connect the fist to the mind that directs it. This is not what the director and screenwriter Paul Schrader had in mind, I think, when he argued that, 'To be of any value, violence must move from vicariousness to artifice. The spectator must be left "disinterested" in the Arnoldian sense, evaluating what he had previously revelled in.'*

In any case, it can frequently feel as if fists have been made redundant by the mechanical and detached damage of firearms – a broad truth that gives rise to an effective cinematic joke in *Raiders of the Lost Ark*. After a prolonged sequence of unarmed combat, in which Harrison Ford has kicked, punched and somersaulted his way through countless turbaned assailants, a brief interlude of calm is ended by the appearance of an enormous Arab wielding a curved sword. Ford sighs in exasperation, pulls his gun from his holster and shoots the man dead, a sudden anachronistic explosion in the midst of this self-consciously vintage mode of combat. The joke partly depends on the discrepancy between the exhausting drudgery of self-defence and the revelation that all along he's had that labour-

Transcendental Style in Film: Ozu, Bresson, Dreyer, Paul Schrader, Da Capo Press, 1988.

saving device on his hip. But it wouldn't work without the audience's dependable nostalgia for older ways of prevailing over an opponent. A kind of mirror-image version of this joke occurs in *Independence Day*. When Will Smith punches an alien attacker, accompanying his blow with the words 'Welcome to Earth', the jubilation of the audience has as much to do with the nature of the weapon as with the relief of a long-deferred retaliation. The scene follows an extended and unequal dogfight between spacecraft and jet fighter, and the punch represents a return to handmade retribution in a world where technological superiority has come to be associated with the enemy. Smith's punch is an emblem of the unequal battle (it draws on the audience's knowledge that aliens have frequently been defeated in the movies by supposedly innocuous substances, although never by something as comically mundane as a smack in the kisser), but it is also an assertion of human resilience. Resistance, it is implied, will not cease while we can still bunch our fingers into a club. The fact that the alien is virtually unconscious anyway doesn't seem to inhibit the audience's pleasure at this moment of primitive triumph.

Smith's punch is a relatively benign variation on the flippant assault – among the coarsest inventions of modern cinema. We have now what was rarer before: the punch entirely *demoralized*, taken out of any context of obligations and duties or ethical judgement. In their casual joking brutality, action heroes remind us of the silent movies' powerful bullies, rather than their ingenious opponents. One of the most shockingly violent scenes of recent years is not, to my mind, the Grand Guignol of Tarantino, rubbing your nose in the sanguine extravagance of the human body, or even Scorsese's virtually unwatchable scenes of mob execution, but an unexceptional moment from a standard Hollywood pot-boiler, *The Specialist*, in which Sharon Stone, encountering mild resistance when she attempts to seize a mobile phone from a matronly passer-by, resolves the matter by punching the woman in the face. The plot supplies her with a mitigation of sorts – the hero will die unless he is warned immediately of imminent danger – but the narrative alibi is not enough to conceal the real motive behind the blow, which is to satisfy the audience's tutored desire for immediate gratification. What has disappeared from the punch in scenes like this is any sense of ambiguity. It is given to us as a cheap evasion of negotiation between opposing desires, and it offers the genuinely dangerous insinuation that violence is a species of wit. In the contemporary Hollywood action movie, no punch is complete without its punchline.

It's sometimes argued that this is amoral violence. But that is to be too casually dismissive of its appeal. In fact, it has a perfectly evolved morality of its own, even if it might not be one that we wish to endorse. It argues that winning is the ultimate good and that compromise is for losers. The modern protagonist does not cut the Gordian knot any more, being generally at a loss for a sword; he or she simply punches out whoever has posed that delaying conundrum. If this offers us the satisfaction of a short cut, it deprives us of something far more valuable: the interrogation of what we desire and fear in our own urges to violence. Over a hundred years the cinematic punch has travelled from literal depiction through a complex and rich symbolism to a brutal literalism again. In both its modern forms – the flippantly indifferent and the notionally troubled – it has impact without weight.

SIZE

Among the mythical encrustations that cinema has accumulated in this century – the sagas of creative endurance, the heroic combats between star and director, the long quest-narratives of would-be stars – there is a small but charming sub-genre. These are stories that you might categorize as Fables of First Encounter, and they describe the meetings that take place between the sophisticated charms of the screen and the unschooled perceptions of remote tribes. The French screen-writer Jean-Claude Carrière offers a typical example in his book *The Secret Language of Film*, in which he tells the story of a team of educational film-makers travelling through Algeria in the 1970s. They had made a film about trachoma, a disease that is transmitted by a fly, and as a result the documentary included several admonitory close-ups of the insect in question.

> After the showing the villagers announced that the film did not concern them. They even seemed surprised that they had been asked to view it.
>
> 'But almost every one of you has trachoma!' a doctor said to them.
>
> 'Yes, but we don't have flies that size here.'

This is an almost canonical example of the genre. The villagers do not react with wonder or alarm but with calm certainty – and that this is a collision of confidence against confidence is crucial to the effect. *They* are puzzled that they have to explain the matter to *us*. There are large elements of self-congratulation in such stories – they often convey a sense of spurious or complacent pride at the superiority of Western knowledge – but there is something else besides. Such stories restore a sense of wonder at what cinema can do with that absolute ground of understanding – the evidence of our own eyes. The tale delivers a sudden reversal of expectations; it offers the giddy pleasure of a convention newly conspicuous to its habitual users, who have become so familiar with its operation that they have effectively forgotten its existence.*

Carrière's version may be representative in another sense, too. It seems entirely possible that it isn't true. Why didn't the villagers say, 'None of us are as small as those people', or 'None of us have heads as big as that', given that the incessant expansion and contraction of objects is also an inescapable element of cinema? Having apparently understood so many pictorial conventions, why was it that they faltered here? There are some plausible answers to such questions – every time somebody walks towards you from a distance, for example, you receive a tutorial in the effects of perspective. No amount of unaided scrutiny, on the other hand, will enlarge a fly to the same degree that a film camera can. Besides, in the mental universe of the villagers a fly was presumably not the sort of object that deserved close inspection anyway; it was simply something to be brushed aside. Indeed, that was precisely what the film sought to change. It wished to transform an inconsiderable object into a considerable one and it unselfconsciously used the cinema's most potent form of alchemy to do it. But if it *was* the case that the villagers applied a literal understanding to the close-up, why then does this story not concern itself with the exclamations of horror and disgust that must have been provoked by such monstrous insects? Why is this not another variation on that most sacred Fable of First Encounter, the reports of audience members bolting from the sight of an oncoming locomotive during early screenings of the Lumière brothers' *L'Arrivée d'un Train à La Ciotat*.

Still, even if the story yields a little under the pressure of thought, it still yields something valuable – a reminder of the camera's marvellous ability to expand and shrink the objects it

---

*There is always a fantasy of return in such stories, a dream of finding again a prelapsarian location from which to see films with uncorrupted eyes, when their strangeness and novelty will once again be more conspicuous to us than their content.

lights upon, an ability that seems to many cinematic initiates to lie at the heart of its seductive power. Even the most sophisticated director was a cinematic innocent once. Martin Scorsese, recalling his first visits to the movies, writes:

> Most of all I was amazed by the size of the images on screen. I would come back and draw what I saw. I made up my own stories, taking my cue from newspaper comic strips and books, and though I didn't realize it at the time, I soon started using close-ups just like they did.*

In very similar vein, Jean Renoir connects the experience of scale in cinema with a childhood sense of awe. In his autobiography he tells of how, while he was acting as producer on the film *Catherine*, he would perform cinematic experiments with the second cameraman during filming:

> I had a notion that the monstrous enlargement of details would help the viewer to enter a dream world. My greatest success in this line was the realisation of my childhood dream, making a close-up of a lizard fill the screen, so that it looked like a ferocious crocodile.†

What I want to consider here are the ways in which the invention of cinema has made primitives of us all, both by effectively ignoring the theories of perception with which it was contemporary and, as in Renoir's case, by performing a kind of magic upon the world.

Size can be created onscreen in two fundamentally different ways – by photographing the very large (an essentially epic procedure that takes place in front of the camera) or by enlarging what is relatively small (an essentially photographic

---

Scorsese on Scorsese, ed. Ian Christie, Faber, London, 1997.
†*My Life and My Films*, Jean Renoir, trs. Norman Denny, Da Capo Press, New York, 1991.

method that takes place inside the camera).* And it is hardly surprising that the early pioneers should have assumed that the readiest way for films to get bigger was by enlarging what they were aimed at – in short, their *scope* (a term that has its origins in the Greek word for target). Here abstract and physical notions come together, the increasing scale of creative ambition finding expression in the sheer bulk of what was filmed. The realization that one no longer need confine oneself to a small theatrical proscenium, as some of the very earliest producers had, meant that the expansion naturally followed the same trajectory – outwards and away from the camera. In *America in the Movies*, his account of fifties popular cinema, Michael Wood equates the epic with the expansion of screen size and his algebra holds good for an earlier time: 'Size means a big screen, and a big screen has to be filled with big things, like cities being burned, like well-attended Roman circuses, like nations on the move.' In truth, 'big things' might just as easily mean 'things made big', but Wood's illustrative list correctly identifies the instinctive resort to the epic of those confronted with expanded cinematic space. The introduction of Cinemascope was a classic instance of a moment when the familiar notions of how to fill a screen became redundant. Panicked by those wide-open spaces, directors suffered a momentary aesthetic agoraphobia and at such times they wanted crowds about them. In some directors the anxiety took a more contemptuous form: 'It's good only for filming great masses in motion,' said Howard Hawks about Cinemascope, a dismissal that probably betrays an uncertainty about how to reshape the dynamics of his own style, which had matured within the more intimate framing of the Academy ratio.† And what Cinemascope and other expanded formats induced in their first users was a kind of

---

*There are occasions, of course, when the two are combined. One of the indispensable effects of early movies was the *matte* shot, in which a miniature model or painting immediately in front of the camera is meticulously aligned with a full-sized location, a teasing combination of the epic and the photographic.
†*Hawks on Hawks*, ed. Joseph McBride, Faber, London, 1998.

regression; they temporarily forgot the sophistications that had evolved over the preceding decades and returned to the pleasures of novelty.*

But the epic solution raises a paradox, even with the greatly expanded space provided by Cinemascope. It is this: in order to fit a very large scene into the limited frame of the projected image it must be diminished. Indeed, the actors within the scene may become barely distinguishable from the swarm of extras that surrounds them. This may not matter during an exodus or a battle, but it can be crucial in other circumstances. Having accustomed themselves to the prodigious status conferred on them by the close attention of the camera, the early film stars were wary of seeing it withdraw again, as it would inevitably have to if it were to capture the vast spaces around them. When Douglas Fairbanks first saw the castle built above Santa Monica Boulevard for *Robin Hood* (then the largest set ever constructed in Hollywood), his astonished pleasure at what his personal fortune had wrought was soon replaced by unease. At the end of his tour of the vast castle he is said to have announced that he was shelving the project. 'I can't compete with that,' Fairbanks told his director Allan Dwan. 'My work is intimate. People know me as an intimate actor. I can't work in a great vast thing like that. What could I do in there?'

Dwan saved the day, reassuring Fairbanks that he could repossess the space with action of a flair and ingenuity that the screen could not previously have accommodated. But Fairbanks's anxiety was shrewd. Nor was he alone in his fear, and the bigger the set the greater was the problem of preserving its grandeur within the frame. In D.W. Griffith's *Intolerance* the constructed locations still have their capacity to dazzle, even in the sadly diminished format of a video copy, but the title cards

---

*My own earliest memory of the cinema is being taken to see *How the West Was Won*, the first film to me made in three-lens Cinerama. I can still recall the gasps that sounded out when the train pounded directly over a camera recessed between the tracks. No one fled from the cinema but most of us, including my parents, flinched backwards. Fifty years on from *L'Arrivée d'un Train à La Ciotat* and the audience could still be made to forget where they were.

betray something like disappointment at how the process of filming had boxed the splendour of those architectural fantasies. An addendum to one of Anita Loos's extravagantly poetic intertitles reads: 'Note. Replica of Babylon's encircling walls, 300 feet in height and broad enough for the passing of chariots.' 'Note,' reads another. 'This hall over a mile in length, imaged after the splendor of an olden day.' In such phrases you hear scholarship edging towards special pleading, the need to reassure the listener with specific measurements. And Allan Dwan clearly felt that Fairbanks was right in the long run. Talking to Kevin Brownlow in 1964, he expressed disenchantment with the grand spectacle:

> Any story worth a damn must be intimate. It must be close to you. It must move you. Size will never move people. They may gasp – and that's it. It's over. You go to New York to see the tall buildings – and once you've seen them, you're satisfied . . . For the average entertainment you need an intimate story – and an intimate story requires good scenes between two people.*

It requires something else besides, something paradoxical. Those two people must fill the screen until all intimacy has been dispelled, at least as regards all those paying voyeurs in the dark. Cinematic intimacy remains a thrilling oxymoron, an erotic ambiguity that depends on the spectator being both within these characters and without them.

It may be that the edge of disappointment contained within all spectacular scenes – the way in which their containment by the screen so quickly depletes their force – is what encourages us to transfer our awe from the imagined circumstances of the story to the real circumstances of its making. Michael Wood rightly notes that the epic onscreen is almost always in part an epic of technical achievement – we marvel not merely at the spectacle but at the very conditions of its existence. What it 'represents' is never simply the building of the pyramids or

*The Parade's Gone By, Kevin Brownlow, University of California Press, 1983.

biblical catastrophe, but the tangible evidence of heroic labour, a myth supported by the miniature *Iliad*s of pre-publicity hype and the introspective *Odyssey*s of production diaries. Even if the spectacle has emerged from the circuits of a computer, we are offered prodigies of number-crunching and programming hours as a kind of substitute for the physical heroism of early movie-making.

Why is it, though, that the massive in cinema loses its impact so quickly? It may help to turn to another primitive vision of the cinema, one so primitive, in fact, that it precedes its invention by some 240 years. In *A Philosophical Inquiry into the Origin of Our Ideas of the Sublime and Beautiful*, Edmund Burke bends himself, among other matters, to the connections between great size and a sense of awe and terror in the audience. In a passage about the effects of obscurity in a work of art or literature he writes:

> Let it be considered that hardly anything can strike the mind with its greatness, which does not make some approach towards infinity; which nothing can do whilst we are able to perceive its bounds; but to see an object distinctly, and to perceive its bounds, is one and the same thing. A clear idea is therefore another name for a little idea.

You don't have to endorse Burke's systematic theory of aesthetic effect in order to find this tremendously illuminating about the tremendous. It certainly helps to explain one of cinema's favourite solutions to the problem of conveying great scale – which is to employ the edge of the frame as an occulting device, an area of darkness that brings into play the potential infinity of imagined space that surrounds every cinema image.

There are numerous examples of this device, in which the length of time it takes fully to reveal to us the size of an object is offered as an alternative measure of its size. Perhaps the best-known example comes from the opening frames of George Lucas's *Star Wars*, in which a fleeing spaceship enters the frame from the top of the screen (effectively above the heads of the audience) and is then pursued by a much larger craft, to the accompaniment of a low seismic rumble (you might not be able to hear a scream in space but apparently engines and laser cannon are perfectly audible). How large it is we do not immediately know, but the sense of an oppressive, intimidatory magnitude remains the finest effect in a film built almost entirely out of effects. Nothing else in the film quite lives up to that opening coup, which is unfortunate as there are another ninety-seven minutes to go. Indeed, time has imposed almost no devaluation on this sequence, as it has on the film's other pioneering technologies, because it is achieved by the simplest means. The overhead angle undoubtedly helps, enlisting a kind of mental triangulation with which we are familiar from the world outside the cinema (to look up to a person or thing is an action always tinged with submission). But the real power of that shot comes from what Burke calls an 'approach to infinity'. We are invited to make a kind of recurrent prediction about the limits of this object, a prediction made impossible by its novelty (we have no obvious experience by which to judge intergalactic Imperial battle cruisers). The result, while the motion lasts, is a continuous upwards revision of our best guess as to its limits, a repeated mental overflowing which carries with it a kind of delicious panic. The effect is powerfully reinforced by the shape of the spaceship, a sharp wedge that has nothing to do with its fictional function (spaceships don't need prows because there are no waves to break), everything to do with its artistic one, which is to drive into the rectangle of the screen. It begins small and grows larger with a geometric progression, and as those angled lines spread sideways in the frame they also point backwards into the unseen space above our heads, vectors that confirm that the longer the motion continues the larger this object will be. Even after their angle has passed out of sight because the ship now occupies the whole width of the frame, we obediently keep them in mind. In short, we perform a projection ourselves, one that neatly reverses the invisible cone of light that has made the image possible in the first place. The sense of mass begins to diminish almost as soon as the full outline of the ship is visible, and it is not simply for the obvious reason that it is now travelling away from us. It has nothing left to reveal and, as Burke points out, the apprehension of an object in its entirety inevitably diminishes it.*

This holds true for more earthbound films, too. When immensity is the value to be represented onscreen, the camera willingly relinquishes its capacity to enclose an object of any scale. (Even the globe can be swallowed whole if you stand far enough back, a fact that was demonstrated by the early Apollo astronauts. Those first pictures of a globe that did not overspill the frame brought home the vulnerability of our planet.)†

This effect depends on deferred revelation, on combining motion and elapsed time in a way that serves as a crude measurement of extension in space. And there is a similar sense of withheld revelation in the cinema's other standard technique for the depiction of immensity, which is to deny the audience any recognizable scale until the very last moment of a long zoom. This is a trick that can be employed to particular effect when we have no earthly means of establishing a sense of relative sizes. In Kubrick's 2001, for example, the director's shot of the circular space station uses a long, slow approach towards a window, an oblong of brilliant light that can finally be seen

*This effect is confirmed even in pastiche. A recent edition of *The X-Files* contained a jokily allusive sequence in which a street light was made to loom with the same portentous vastness. Only when the camera pulled back far enough did it become clear that it was not a spaceship but a banal piece of street furniture.
†Naturally there are other ways of using the enclosure of the frame. That famous opening of John Ford's *The Searchers*, for example, presents audiences with an artificially diminished view – the open door of the homestead through which only a narrow fragment of the exterior landscape can be glimpsed. The inside of the cabin is in deep black shadow, a rectangular mask that cramps the screen so that when the camera tracks forward through the door the effect is as if the projected image had suddenly dilated. Many years later this same vertiginous effect was used in early films for Imax cinemas, a format that was almost exclusively concerned with overwhelming its audience through sheer mass.

to contain tiny moving figures. Suddenly, comprehensible magnitude is restored to an object first seen floating in uncalibrated space. And it is important to the effect here that we are presented with that bodily measurement *too late*, only when the boundaries of the object to be measured have long ago disappeared beyond the edges of the screen, outside our calculating grasp.

Ridley Scott employs a very similar device in *Blade Runner*, his projection of the film noir sensibility on to a dystopian future. The camera moves forward through the murky, flare-lit cityscape, closing in on one of the massive ziggurat apartment blocks to reveal a tiny figure silhouetted in a window. The next cut makes it clear that it is Harrison Ford, pacing the gloomy interior of his apartment.* So a camera motion that is inseparably associated with magnification ends not in the realm of the microscopic but with the human figure, and we understand the implication at once: this space does not merely dwarf us, it makes us almost invisible. *Blade Runner* is oddly preoccupied with such penetrating motions – perhaps because its plot concerns a crucial distinction that is invisible to the naked eye – and it takes to a finer level of definition than any predecessor the dizzying experience of a successive revelation of particular detail. Though these effects precede the widespread popularization of fractal theory, that is essentially the experience they present us with, of details nested within detail, invisible to our eyes until they have been magnified sufficiently by the camera. And though this is a modern experience, it is not simply a twentieth-century one; its vertigo belongs to the age of the microscope, which dizzyingly enlarged the territory of the living. When Constantijn Huygens writes of the way in which this instrument abolished the complacent certainty of human scale,

*There is an additional twist here, though, because although his vista is fantastic, it is also earthbound. This Stygian panorama is built on the foundations of what is already an established cliché of urban excess – the lights of Los Angeles seen from the Hollywood Hills. That famous perspectival grid, combining fine and distinct grain in the foreground with an indistinguishable haze of light on the horizon, offers every visitor a tour-bus version of Pascal's infinite spaces.

his example has an almost cinematic quality to it, and the same sense of new territory opened up for the eye's exploration: 'For example: a city gate as we now see it is but a mere crevice, compared to a crevice as seen through the magnifying lenses, which looks like a huge gate.'* Huygens acknowledges the relativism of vision that is exploited by Kubrick and Scott in their films, the way in which a spinning thigh bone can occupy the same amount of screen space as an immense man-made structure revolving in orbit around the moon.

Such motions of enlargement are almost always associated in film with an amplification of truth. Consider two well-known examples: the sequence in Michelangelo Antonioni's *Blow-Up* in which David Hemmings repeatedly enlarges his photographs of a park to reveal what appears to be evidence of a murder, and a similar sequence in *Blade Runner* in which Harrison Ford uses computer imaging to delve into the depths of a snapshot for evidence. Neither of these passages is unambiguous – Antonioni hints at a derangement of vision and takes great care to make his evidence inconclusive, while Scott's film cheats with its angles (the 'enlargements' involve an impossible shift of perspective). But both sequences work from the underlying assumption that understanding will increase in direct proportion to optical resolution, that we need to go beyond the superficial appearance of things.

This is by no means the only way we have of understanding the world, as our clichés of comprehension remind us. We can also take a few steps back to get everything into perspective. But the cinema greatly favours getting closer to the object. Although there are instances in film in which a retreating movement reveals a larger truth, they are as often employed for comic purposes as for an arousal of awe. (Think, for instance, of a close shot of a man relaxing on a lilo, sipping at an elaborately garlanded cocktail. The camera then pulls back to reveal that a huge expanse of open ocean surrounds him on all

*From *The Art of Describing*, Svetlana Alpers, John Murray, 1983.

sides.) And such jocular movements are greatly outnumbered by scenes in which a zoom or some other form of advancing motion opens the way to greater understanding. There is a complicated intellectual history behind such an assumption – which has to do with the growing prestige of the eye as the foremost scientific organ of sense – but there is a simple human one too. In its respect for the revelatory power of the zoom, cinema acknowledges what has long been a bodily instinct in most viewers, even before the invention of the microscope or the magnifying lens: obscurity in an image usually prompts us to bring it closer to us or to approach it ourselves. And even if our position is fixed, another kind of enlargement is still possible. In an interview about his work with Antonioni on *Beyond the Clouds*, the German director Wim Wenders expressed his distaste for the zoom. 'This instrument is like a red rag to a bull for me,' he said, 'precisely because it doesn't translate the look of the human eye, but represents a technical look.'* However much one might share his distaste for a crude overuse of the zoom, his line of argument is flawed, because the human eye is an organ inseparable from the visual cortex of the brain. And the brain can certainly zoom, even if the cornea and the retina cannot. 'The mental lens works like this with variety,' wrote Eisenstein, praising a vivid passage of description from Da Vinci's journals, 'it enlarges the scale or diminishes it, adjusting as faithfully as a film camera to varying frame requirements.'†

For cinema then, the zoom – and its logical culmination the close-up – offer a visible model of mental concentration. Like mental concentration, the close-up is crucially a combination of enhancement *and* exclusion, and it is one of the pleasures of the zoom that it shows us that process of distillation in progress. As the zoom proceeds, what is extraneous and peripheral is visibly forced outwards from the edge of the frame to permit

*From an interview in *Sight and Sound*, July 1996.
†'The Film Sense', Sergei Eisenstein, Harcourt Brace, 1969.

the centre of the image to grow in potency. Indeed, the *Oxford English Dictionary*'s definition of 'concentration' can be applied without any adjustment to the effects of a cinematic zoom – '1. To bring to or towards a common centre or focus ... 2. *Chem.* To increase the strength of a solution by contraction of its volume.' Just as with mental concentration, the close-up temporarily surrenders an apprehension of the world at large in return for a greatly enlarged apprehension of one of its details.

It isn't very surprising, then, that penetrating motions of the camera occur from very early in the cinema's history. There is a justly celebrated shot in King Vidor's *The Crowd* in which one uninterrupted motion takes us from the fulminating streets of Manhattan, up the side of a vast skyscraper, through one of its innumerable, indistinguishable windows to the hero of the film, sitting, like hundreds of men around him, at a desk in the middle of a field of desks. Even earlier there is Griffith's famous slanting descent into the heart of the Babylon set, a movement that traverses the immense space of his set to finish on figures that were initially indistinguishable. Like Vidor's shot it achieves a paradoxical effect of diminution out of enlargement, reminding us how negligible and minute the human figure is within such enormous spaces.* But this shrinking of the living figure, its conversion into a microscopic being in a world of unnerving scale, is not the manipulation of human scale one would conventionally associate with the cinema. Mostly, the screen magnified its actors. There were giants in those days and it was the powerful geometry of projected light that created them. Initially, at least, there was a kind of perceptual embarrassment at the transformations the camera could effect – it is intriguing how often departures from life-size (either through

*Griffith's shot is, incidentally, an imitation – effectively an upended version of what was known at the time of filming as a *Cabiria* shot, after Giovanni Pastrone's hugely influential Italian epic, which introduced the use of long, diagonal tracking movements to emphasize the three-dimensional extent of his own enormous sets. *Cabiria* shots were extremely fashionable in 1915 and 1916, when Griffith was making *Intolerance*.

close-up or insert shots) are explicitly linked to existing technologies of magnification, as if the disruption of the camera's
distance from its subjects needed some kind of narrative alibi.
G.A. Smith's *As Seen Through a Telescope* (1901) cuts from a
long shot of a man looking through a telescope at a woman
being helped on to a bicycle to a close-up of her ankle, which
is filmed with a circular iris to confirm that this is his point of
view. An earlier film by the same director, *Grandma's Reading
Glass* (1900), in which a small boy plays with his grandmother's
magnifying glass, was accompanied by an explanatory note in
the distribution company's catalogue: 'The conception is to
produce on screen the various objects as they appeared to Willy
while looking through the glass in their enormously enlarged
form.' But if it was felt at first that close-ups needed some kind
of internal explanation, both directors and audiences learnt
the convention with great speed. Within a couple of years,
scopophilia, a delirious pleasure in looking, needs no props and
the apparatus can be dispensed with.

Despite that liberty, though, optical devices of enlargement
remain important to directors for many years to come. In Eisenstein's *The Battleship Potemkin*, a quarter of a century on from
Smith's commercial novelty, the crucial inspection of the rotten
meat is preceded by a medium shot of the spectacles of the
ship's doctor, followed by an extreme close-up in which they
are folded into an impromptu magnifying lens, with the doctor's
eye looking through it at the audience (as if we were putrefying
meat, in other words). This is clearly not an explanatory device;
Eisenstein could confidently rely on his audience understanding
that the huge pair of glasses being folded are those we have just
seen taken off the doctor's nose. But the image effectively sets
the proud acuity of cinema – its forensic ability to demonstrate the facts of the case – against a wilful and wicked myopia.
Smirnov looks closely, sees precisely what we see (the reverse-
angle cut is by this time a well-established convention for point
of view) and he then denies the manifest truth. 'These are not
maggots,' he declares in the title card, continuing to explain

that they are merely fly's eggs which can be washed off with water. This assertion is immediately contradicted by a close-up of the maggots' squirming vitality. Our outrage and disgust at this point is neither just political nor physical; it is epistemological, the affront of having the evidence of our own eyes so flatly disavowed. Much later in the film, as the officers are being thrown overboard, there is an uncomfortably vindictive title – 'Down to feed the maggots' – which specifically recalls this moment, and Eisenstein inserts a close-up of Smirnov's spectacles dangling from a rope – an object whose misuse has offered a symbol of the old regime's mendacious treachery. It is in keeping with both these close-ups that one of the climactic shots in the Odessa Steps sequence shows a shattered spectacle lens on the face of a woman protester, a Tsarist bullet having destroyed the instrument of proletarian clear-sightedness. In neither case is there any sense that these corrective lenses imply a sense of deficient vision in those who possess them; they are instead emblems of an ability to discriminate between false and true appearances, and in that sense they are visible representatives of the transparent and invisible lens by which both images are made possible in the first place, that of the camera.

In his own writings, Eisenstein is quite clear about the distinction between such purposeful close-ups and the American model. Indeed, in his essay 'Film Form', he makes a case for a specifically native – that is, Soviet – aesthetic:

> We refer to the close-up, or as we speak of it, the 'large scale'. This distinction in principle begins with an essence that exists in the term itself. We say: an object or face is photographed in 'large scale', i.e. large. The American says: near or 'close-up'. We are speaking of the qualitative side of the phenomenon, linked with its meaning (just as we speak of a large talent, that is, of one which stands out by its significance, from the general line, or of large print to emphasise that which is particularly essential or significant). Among Americans the term is attached to *viewpoint*. Among us *to the value of what is seen*.

83

Eisenstein insists that Soviet cinema is doing something mark-edly different from Griffith, using the magnitude of the image 'not only and not so much to show or to present as to signify, to give meaning, to designate'. This is, it should be pointed out, unfair to American films, which had already demonstrated an ability to move beyond the merely explanatory and use inserts for symbolic or poetic purposes, but it does indicate the appro-priative passion that Eisenstein brings to the device, his determination to bend the world to his own artistic purposes. The close-up, he says elsewhere, gives us 'an abstraction of the lifelike'. Eisenstein's translator may have done us a service here – I don't know whether the ambiguity exists in the Russian original but in English the word 'abstraction' is perfectly poised between taking and giving. The close-up not only confers upon objects the quality of an abstract concept, divorcing them from their mundane practical purposes, but is an exploitation of the world's rich resources of meaning – significance can be abstracted from the 'lifelike' just as coal is abstracted from a mine.

Eisenstein isn't the only director to make use of onscreen lenses as an allusion to the moral powers of vision. In *La Règle du Jeu*, Jean Renoir explicitly refers to the telescope as a device for delving to the heart of a matter. Out walking in the country-side, Christine looks through a telescope at a squirrel, an animal that fills the screen in the subsequent point-of-view shot. 'With a telescope you can penetrate the private life of that squirrel,' says her companion. This isn't simply an irony in the making (for in the very next moment Christine swings the telescope down to pierce her own private life, seeing the Marquis in the distance kissing his mistress); it is an implicit plea on behalf of the scrutinizing power of the camera – its ability to detect truth beneath appearance. The squirrel fills the frame just as Christine's face does in the reaction shot that follows her revel-ation. As she looked at the squirrel so we look at her and a kind of visual syllogism is established, with the invisible lens of the camera as the unstated connection. It's typical that Renoir should be fully aware of the contrary argument. In *Boudu Saved from Drowning*, produced seven years earlier, the eponymous tramp is first seen through a telescope as he walks alongside the Seine. 'Look at him. Isn't he marvellous!' says his observer, drawing attention to the distancing effect of a telescope, which can bring us the picturesque surfaces of a *clochard* without the smell or belligerence that accompanies the person. This is the great central joke of *Boudu*, a comedy about the re-education of sentimental perceptions, and it alludes, too, to the dangers of sentiment always prevalent in cinema – another kind of vision in which the objects of our admiration or affection are held safely at a distance from us. Film always leans towards prettification even when its images are conventionally ugly, because it always protects us from the consequences of what it depicts, and despite its implicit rebuke to such distortion, *Boudu* itself still has the power to charm us with its central character.

Even so, despite such percipient dissent, the idea that the camera is a device of revelatory optic power rapidly becomes a commonplace. 'The camera will see nothing that it is not shown,' wrote Cocteau, defending the unblinking honesty of the medium. 'It cruelly and faithfully records the least of our faults. On the luminous screen it will multiply them through a dangerous magnifying glass.'* 'The camera's more than a recorder, it's a microscope,' said Elia Kazan. 'It penetrates, it goes into people.' Such remarks are very familiar and they assume, almost without exception, that the magnification will always result in a larger truth.

At the same time, the idea of a higher truth is often associated with disenchantment. The opening of David Lynch's *Blue Velvet* might be taken as exemplary. With its enormously magnified descent into that epitome of suburban respectability – the bland expanse of an immaculate lawn – it reveals a hidden world of monsters, an experience that had been at the heart of

The Art of Cinema, a collection of Cocteau's writings and speeches, trs. Robin Buss, Marion Boyars, 1993.

microscopy at least a hundred years earlier. 'Nothing could be more horrible,' wrote one visitor to a London exhibition hall featuring displays on the solar microscope, 'no more frightful, devilish figures could possibly be invented – than the disgusting water animalculae which we daily swallow.'*

There arises something of a difficulty here. How is it that an effect that so steadily – so scientifically, you might say – deprives us of our illusions can also reinforce them? Just what kind of optical instrument is the motion-picture camera, that it can move so freely between the revelation of concealed truth and the creation of delusory magic? It is possible to find some answers in the human face. Some of the very earliest close-ups were those of actors' features, the camera lured into an unaccustomed proximity by the most legible object in its field of vision (far more legible than the intertitles, given the often illiterate condition of its audiences). Not simply the most legible either, but the most attractive, an object whose magnetic compulsion of the gaze is coded into our very biology. It has been said that D.W. Griffith first used the close-up because he was so enchanted with the beauty of one of his female stars that he wished to share it more generously with his audience, but then it has also been said that D.W. Griffith was the first director to use the close-up, a 'fact' that is demonstrably untrue.

It wasn't even the case that Griffith excelled in the use of close-up, even if his exploration of the device excited much emulation in his colleagues (and in Eisenstein, who grasped its poetic potential more fully). Griffith's close-ups offer a kind of privilege of proximity that often interrupts his narrative flow, such as his close framings of an actress's features – images to which that overworked adjective 'iconic' can be applied with some justice, given the religiose droop that the director often favoured. Or they present the viewer with a rather crude metonymy, using a part of the body to stand in for the whole,

*The Shows of London, Richard D. Altick, Harvard University Press, Cambridge, Mass., 1978.

such as the close-up of a mother's hand plucking at her baby's clothes after the child has been officiously abducted by charitable busybodies in *Intolerance*.*

For the actor, such enlargements of the face were understandably intoxicating, a literal measure of their degree of magnificence within the screen's hierarchy of importance. Jean Renoir, writing about Raimu ('perhaps the greatest French actor of the century') describes his childlike understanding of this element of film. 'All he knew about the cinema was that a close-up showed the details of a face. During shooting he would constantly say to the cameraman, "Make me big." '† Perhaps Raimu knew more than Renoir was ready to concede, because he certainly appears to have grasped that there is a distinction between 'greatness' and the quality of being 'big'. Where the theatre has great actors, the cinema has big stars (or 'massive' or 'huge') and it is impossible to dissect the latter term in such a way that the magnitude of a career can be separated from the size of the image onscreen.

There may be a cost, as in all Faustian contracts. Garbo once famously said that 'the close-up had almost destroyed me', and Tony Curtis, in a recent interview with his daughter,†† describes at least one effect of such a transfiguration. 'It was astounding how critical I became of my looks when I saw my face blown up thirty-five feet.' The screen's appetite for beauty follows at least in part from the enlarged territory for appreciation it offers; there is, in square footage alone, so much more to admire. But the practical effect onscreen is often contradictory. The screen magnifies beauty in ways that are not straightforward; indeed, that often involve a mendacious evasion of clear sight. Cosmetics necessarily had to reinforce the fallible

*There is a whole essay to be written about cinema's use of the hand as a register of bodily or psychological sensation – from the clenched fists of *The Battleship Potemkin* to the clutching fingers of countless decorous orgasms.
†From *My Life and My Films*, Jean Renoir, trans. Norman Denny, Da Capo Press, New York, 1991.
††*Projections 5*, Faber, London, 1996.

beauty of some stars and early cameramen knew that, with older performers in particular, something had to be interposed between the cruel sharpness of the lens and vulnerable flesh. Diffusion lenses were frequently used, a voluntary surrender of clarity for protective purposes, but some cameraman preferred a gauze with two holes burnt in it by a cigarette, a semi-transparent mask that veiled the accumulated flaws of skin and muscle but allowed the eyes – those Dorian Grays of the face – to shine without impediment. (There is here a mirror-image paradox to set alongside that with which we began. Just as the epic shot must shrink a genuinely grandiose reality in order to fit it onscreen, the close-up can diminish a reputation for physical perfection by enlarging the grounds on which it rests.)

It seems perfectly emblematic that Tony Curtis's experience of enlargement should have been prefigured during his war-time service as a naval signalman. The inside of the signalling light contained a huge mirror to amplify the beam: 'When I stood in front of that mirror, it was to die for. I went from this diminutive, charming, handsome Jewish boy to this movie giant. I looked at myself. My face was magnified three times in that mirror but in proportion, perfect.' That his two accounts contradict each other – magnification leading both to an uneasy awareness of imperfection and to that complacent 'perfect' – is to the point. The screen is a dangerous plane of existence for just that reason, a thin sheet that separates luminous aggrandizement and brilliant exposure.

Burke is useful again here, and this time not because he anticipates a truth of cinema but because he confidently asserts something that film has since proved false. In *A Philosophical Inquiry* he has this to say: 'The large and gigantic, though very compatible with the sublime is contrary to the beautiful. It is impossible to suppose a giant the object of love.' This is intriguing because – although it is true when Burke writes it – the experience of cinema has greatly undermined it. We *do* suppose the giants of the screen to be objects of love because it is in the nature of cinema to allow them both immensity and

emotion.* This is achievable in no other visual art form that I can think of, partly because most alternatives are static but also because the sheer physical mass of a statue is likely to invoke feelings of inferiority in us. A statue of a person that was thirty-five feet high would be monumental, intimidating, a coercive argument for power. It could not express the vulnerability that is essential to any convincing depiction of love. But the screen gives us size without mass, and immensity here arouses quite different feelings in us. It may be that there is a biological component in our emotional responses to the faces we see onscreen and particularly to those seen in extreme close-up. I have in mind here not our inherited reactions to expressions of joy or grief or terror, but the rather subtler question of how much territory a face occupies in our visual field. Cinema close-ups offer a visual experience that is otherwise only encountered in conditions of true intimacy. Clearly the recent dwindling of the cinema screen for technical and commercial reasons has made this harder to sense, but even in a cinema with a relatively small screen a large close-up will expand the face of the actor to a size that would, if the person was actually before you in life, place them well within the cordon of your private space.†
It is hardly surprising that it is so easy to fall in love with screen stars, because we so often see them as if their breath were whispering on our lips. This effect is not a necessary condition of infatuation with the presences onscreen, otherwise the diminished stars of television could not exercise the emotional power they do, but it seems likely that it helps to amplify the

*It might be objected here that we don't really think of screen stars as giants. They don't exist in a monstrous world; they exist in a simulation of ours that has been projected. For most of a film we aren't even consciously aware of the actual size of the image. But I would counter that it *is* part of the impact of actors onscreen that they are 'gigantic', that they overwhelm us and face us down.
†If this sounds implausible, you can easily test it for yourself the next time you are at the cinema. Even in medium shot, an actor's head will often be several times as big as that of the person sitting immediately in front of you. In extreme close-up the screen brings the human face well inside the average person's ability to focus – that is, if a face occupied that much of your visual field in real life, it would be an intimate blur.

speculative adoration some stars arouse in us – that blend of gazing and dreaming that the cinema so powerfully evokes.

There may be occasions, then, when intimacy is much more important than legibility. Although I suggested earlier that the human face is a peculiarly readable object, and although this remains true in the innumerable reaction shots with which films spell out a set of psychological relationships, it isn't very long before a self-consciously illegible close-up comes into existence (illegible, that is, within the ostensible narrative of the film). At such times the face becomes writable rather than readable. When Josef Von Sternberg presents Marlene Dietrich in close-up in *The Scarlet Empress*, at the point when she has just given birth to her child, he depicts her behind a netted veil. And it is a striking feature of this scene that the lens focuses on the net rather than on the face behind it. You find yourself looking at the skewed grid of the veil as if at a pixellated screen, a mosaic of light and shade which taken together amounts to a hallowed object. And this shot does not sit in any explanatory or symbolic relation to what precedes it. It might be possible, I suppose, to argue that the net is intended to represent Catherine's ensnare-ment in the intrigues of the Russian court, but you would have to ignore the fact that this is for her a moment of liberation rather than enclosure (as the mother of the heir to the throne she now has greatly expanded powers and opportunities). You could alternatively argue that the tantalizing withholding of focus suggests the character's essential enigma. Dietrich's face floats in some indefinable plane behind the net, unreachable through its narrow mesh. But the scene doesn't plausibly feel as if it would fit either of these explanations. It feels like an interlude for reverent looking, an undefined gaze that mimics a state of unfocused, uncritical contemplation. In such scenes we are forcefully reminded that the modern sense of magnifying – an act of optical enlargement that enhances our ability to make fine judgements – has crowded out a far more ancient meaning – that of extolling or praising something, an experience that does not include the idea of such discriminations. When Christians are asked to 'magnify the Lord's name', it is not an invitation to get their microscopes out and look for flaws.

Others have shared Von Sternberg's almost delirious desire to escape, however briefly, from the insistent demand of narrative that we always be moving on.* In his autobiography, Renoir wrote:

> I am ready to bear with the most tedious film if it gives me a close-up of an actress I like, and in my passion for the close-up I have sometimes inserted perfectly irrelevant sequences in my films simply because they allowed me scope for a really good one.

This is entirely in keeping with Renoir's stated passion for magical enlargement, but he knew that he had to take into account a more literal appetite on the part of the public. 'What mattered to me was a fine close-up,' he repeats later. 'It so happened that if they were to accept a close-up, the public had to be given a story. I bowed to the necessity but with reluctance.' There is almost certainly an element of performance in this passage, of the director setting his own delirious aestheticism against the coarser appetites of the audience, but there is a truth too. While the remark doesn't exactly square with Renoir's commitment to the virtues of deep-focus *mise en scène* and long, uncut scenes, it marks the presence of the primitive within an autodidact of cinema.

What Renoir refers to here, anyway, is less a conscious demand on the part of the audience for justification than a trained response that they cannot lightly abandon. The audience can hardly be blamed if they had come to understand a close-up as a coded text to be interpreted, because legibility (or in some cases a lecture) were so frequently what close-ups were about in early cinema. 'Inserts are made so that you can read them,' Jack Warner declared bluntly (using the Hollywood term

---

*They are unlikely, though, to match him in the intensity of his purpose. He once claimed that he would like to project his films upside down so that the audience could relish their formal qualities without the distraction of a storyline.

for interpolated close-ups).* This uncomplicated diktat was passed on to Don Siegel when he joined the Warner Brothers Insert Department, which produced close-ups to the requirements of directors too busy to shoot them for themselves, or even, on some occasions, for film editors who would decide what was required in the finished sequence. The division of labour hints at the ancestral origins of many Hollywood close-ups, which belong not to the visual realm controlled by the director but to the explanatory realm of the title-writer. And often Warner's remark was literally the case. The close-up would give the audience access to a piece of text whose contents they needed to see – a telegram, a letter, or a medical prognosis. Even when no words were visible, though, his description has metaphorical force; in the close-up there is almost always a task of decipherment at hand.

This doesn't mean, of course, that the use of the close-up is static in historical terms. Putting it crudely, you might say that the trajectory of the close-up over time arcs from simple answers to suggestive interrogation. It may grow out of the clarifying interventions of silent cinema, those moments when a written title performs a pre-emptive retaliation against the feared misunderstanding of the audience. But it soon matures from being an answer to a predicted question ('What is he looking at?' 'What's in the letter?') into something far more important for cinema's construction of meaning. It blossoms into a question in its own right – by which I mean that it asks the audience to resolve a mystery. We have to ask ourselves where exactly we can place *this* piece of visual meaning into the unstable structure we build as the film proceeds. A close-up is always a shard of reality, one that, in this case, is not destined to be fitted back into the whole it originally came from, but to be appropriated for the film's evolving mosaic of such fragments. And in many cases it is the audience that is required to transform it from an unadopted, orphan detail into something meaningful. It is usually unwise

*A Siegel Film, Don Siegel, Faber, London, 1996.

to confuse age with progress in the arts but I would stand by the prejudices of value in the terms 'mature' and 'blossom' used here. We need to remember that both forms of close-up – the explanatory and the suggestive – are simultaneously present for most of cinema's history but we can still say that the flower is better than the bud. In the best close-ups you can see that a functional tool has evolved into an expressive instrument.

This trajectory could be described in another way – as a gradual toughening of the questions asked of the viewer. Some questions are easier to answer than others, evidently. If we see a man reading a telegram we know that the subsequent close-up is a straightforward device of legibility. If a woman opens a letter and looks shocked it is likely that the consequent close-up ('My darling, I cannot marry you. I am betrothed to another') effectively answers its own question. But even in the most controlled close-up there is likely to be something superfluous, simply because photography always takes more from the world than is needed for its employer's immediate purposes. The point can be illustrated with two close-ups from Alfred Hitchcock's *Suspicion*, a thriller that depends on the unreliability of appearances. The first of them occurs very near the beginning of the film, when Cary Grant and Joan Fontaine meet in a railway compartment, and it shows us the tickets they respectively hand over to the inspector, a repeated sequence that confirms that Grant is not entitled to be travelling first class while Fontaine is. The second of them comes a little later in the film and shows us Fontaine's handbag being snapped shut, just after Grant has moved to kiss her while they are out walking in the countryside. Though both scenes share a technical similarity in terms of lens aperture and focal length, there is a marked difference between them. It lies in the narrative redundancy of the image, usually the best marker an audience has that something more is expected of them than mere recognition. Now, I would want to concede right away that such distinctions can never be entirely clear cut. The tickets, for example, aren't simply informative, indeed cannot remain so once they have been placed in the

monstrance of Hitchcock's frame. They take on a halo of insinuation, one that finds a visible expression in the faint change
in image quality and the perceptible snag in the rhythms of the
editing, which briefly depart from a realistic continuity.

These images do not simply establish that the ticket inspector
is right and Grant mistaken (or disingenuous in his protests of
confusion). First of all, the prominence of the print makes it
clear that error is simply not a possibility. Unless Grant's vision
is somehow deficient compared to ours then he must have
known he was misusing his ticket (and unless specifically alerted
otherwise, we automatically assume a parity of vision in the
cinema, that the characters onscreen can see what we can see).
A sense of his untrustworthiness is unavoidable. Second, those
two terms – first class and third class – linked by apposition
with Fontaine and Grant have an effect, however subliminal,
on our responses to the characters they play. They explicitly
play out the tragic arithmetic of the film, which goes on to
demonstrate that love or infatuation can place an equal sign
between figures of very different worth (it remains a tragedy, I
think, despite its much-debated 'happy' ending). Above all,
though, the close-ups make immediate sense as being presented
for our greater information – without them we wouldn't be
able to judge exactly how far Grant's duplicity stretched. Strictly
speaking we don't need to see Joan Fontaine's ticket at all, even
though we are given far more time to read it, which is one
reason why its presence helps to confirm the insinuating force
of those two descriptions.

There is no equally obvious narrative justification for the
sudden close-up of Fontaine's purse snapping shut, a scene that
follows an ambiguous struggle between her and Grant. (When
seen in long shot it is impossible to tell whether he is attacking
or embracing her, but everything in the scene prejudices us
towards the first interpretation, including the shrill, alarmed
dissonance of Franz Waxman's music.) She resists his intimacies,
which include a seductive pantomime of penetration, when
Grant touches Fontaine, pushing his finger into that vulnerable

divot where the neck meets the collarbone.* The head-and-shoulders two-shot in which Grant bends towards Fontaine's face to kiss her is ended by her recoil and a very brief close-up of her hands snapping shut the clasp of her handbag. It's difficult to construe this movement exactly but it is as assertive as it is spasmodic, a determination as much as a reflexive flinch. And yet there is unquestionably an innuendo in the brief top-billing given to this accessory (it is an obvious but significant fact about close-ups that they require everything else, however important, to leave the screen). There are no other close-ups in the scene, not of her hair – the object of Grant's teasing, impudent attention – or even of that arousing cleft below her neck, so whatever else we understand about that bag, we know that it contains within its depths some oblique significance. And you hardly need to know the long cultural history of the purse as a substitutive metaphor for the vagina to feel, at some level at least, the charge of frigid closure that Hitchcock makes. He has found a screenable image not just for sexual panic but for vaginismus – an image that draws its power from the difficulty we have in determining with any certainty whether the gesture is involuntary or willed. Immediately afterwards, Fontaine returns to her home and overhears her parents talking about her through an open window. 'I suppose she is rather spinsterish,' says the mother, agreeing with the father's prediction that she is unlikely ever to marry. Fontaine turns to kiss Grant in a sudden move of defiance, an impulse at odds with her earlier gesture of pinched refusal.

It is a commonplace to say of close-ups that they are included for reasons of emphasis, but such a scene brings home the rhetorical origins of the word. An emphasis is not merely a stress, though that is what it has come to mean in common

*Grant provides himself with an alibi by praising the beauty of her 'uccipital mapillary', and when she asks what he is referring to he touches her in explanation. I take it the anatomical gobbledegook is further evidence of the character's unreliability because this feature is actually called the suprasternal notch – under which name it appears in *The English Patient*, in the scene where Ralph Fiennes lovingly traces the topography of Kristin Scott-Thomas's body.

usage; it is a figure of speech in which *more is implied than is actually said*. More instructively still it derives from the Greek word for 'appearance' – as opposed to substance, that is. There could scarcely be a more appropriate term for the way in which a close-up offers us a mediation between a photographic fidelity to the surfaces of the world and the manipulative vision of the artist. Hitchcock is a genius of emphasis, a rhetorician who asks us to lend him our eyes. In an early hymn of praise to the director, Jean-Luc Godard wrote:

> Let me make myself plain. It is not in terms of liberty and destiny that cinematographic *mise en scène* is measured, but in the ability of genius to batten on objects with constant invention, to take nature as a model, to be infallibly driven to embellish things which are insufficient.*

What Godard describes is the writer's opportunism, and his remark reminds us that in its combination of literary manipulation and optical magnification the cinema produces a quite new experience, one that had not previously been accessible to a paying public.

Victorian customers had been able to experience the alternative worlds of the microscopic and the macroscopic. The solar microscope projected its images so that a large audience could view them simultaneously and the development of the oxy-hydrogen microscope made such displays independent of the weather. At Stanley's Rooms in Old Bond Street, those looking for edifying entertainment could find science fiction in a glass of water (the water of the time being particularly well populated). At the other extreme the vast had long been accessible, too – in the cult of immensity that led to an inflationary spiral in the size of canvases. (In 1815 the British Institution offered a prize of £1,000 for a canvas 16 feet by 25 feet expressing in 'allegorical spirit the triumph of Wellington', a

*From *Godard on Godard: Critical Writings by Jean-Luc Godard*, Da Capo Press, 1988.

prize that was eventually won by a picture measuring 35 by 22 feet.) This taste for expansive vistas was also reflected in the popularity of the diorama, a form of representation that offered pleasures very similar to the detailed spectaculars of the wide-screen epic, including its passion for panning movements. But the magnifying exercises of the cinema occupy an intermediate space in continuum of spectacle, one that was essentially vacant until cinema arrived. The oxyhydrogen microscope made monsters out of microbes, allowing us to see what would otherwise be invisible, while the vast historical paintings used a suitably grand and intimidating space in which to deploy its unfamiliar heroes (or unseen sights). Cinema, by contrast, could transform what was banal by reason of its visual familiarity. Cinema makes a mediocre world – in its old sense as something that is neither big nor small – into a world of heroic actors. Still life had done this to a certain extent already, deploying mundane objects as moral emblems, but it rarely magnified its subject matter to any great degree. Indeed, we might usefully ask the question why painters had not walked through the open door that led to enlargement. Why are there no Dutch still lifes in which grapes are shown a foot across, when magnification was at the heart of much Dutch visual culture? Such an image would not have been technically inconceivable, but something seems to have made it aesthetically undesirable, some embarrassment about the implications of exceeding the visible world.

Cinema suffers from no such inhibitions – or at least very rapidly shakes them off. And this is partly because it has no choice; the extreme close-up is one of the few means the medium has of recovering the tunnel vision of literature. That is: any object not actively described in a book will be effectively invisible (conjurable, certainly, by an imaginative or a perverse reader, but not unavoidably present). In film, on the other hand, the description spills over with extraneous matter, every element of which may compete for our notoriously skittish attention. This is a perpetual hazard for directors – there will always be those who find themselves thinking about bathroom fittings during the shower scene from *Psycho*. But close-up at least offers the director a way of corralling our wayward perception, restoring some of prose's enviable tyranny over the mind's eye. The close-up can feel so much like a gift to our eyes, a beautiful *largesse*, that it is easy to forget that it is usually a matter of taking things away from us, withholding sight in such a way that the director's authority over our imaginations is reinforced. (Though it's worth noting that in the actual practice of the Hollywood studio system the large close-up or insert shot became a place of refuge for a particular kind of subversive poetry, a protective enclave where the surreal and the fantastic could flourish, in the midst, as it were, of a larger conformity to the classical Hollywood style. In *Dark Victory*, for example, Bette Davis's realization that she will go blind is conveyed to the audience by a point-of-view insert of her medical notes: the phrase 'Prognosis Negative' lifts off the page and expands to fill the screen, an expressive touch that sits within a far more conventional movie.)

This poetic coercion operates in various ways, many of which are direct manipulations of our prejudices of perception. Cinema, for example, can easily play with our hierarchies of dependence – the learnt instinct by which an ordinary observer will usually see a mosquito as attached to an elephant rather than the elephant to the mosquito. These orderings have their place in the world but in film they are always prone to disruption. In filming *Notorious*, Hitchcock had a giant coffee cup constructed so that he could film the object (which contains poison) in what appeared to be extreme close-up alongside Ingrid Bergman's head in medium shot – an otherwise impossible combination.* In the resulting image she is thus dwarfed by an object designed to fit into her hand, so that it becomes

---

*This was a technique he resorted to several times in his career. *Spellbound*, made just a year earlier, contains a scene in which a giant hand and revolver were constructed so that Hitchcock could create the effect of deep focus in the point-of-view scene in which Leo G. Carroll shoots himself and Ingrid Bergman is seen in the background.

clear that she is subject to *its* force rather than the other way round. (Hitchcock had used an almost identical shot eight years earlier in *The Lady Vanishes*, though in that case the actors' brandy glasses loom without menace – it is a visual gimmick rather than an effective trick of melodrama.) In a similar way, the implied ability of an object to command the attention of the camera (and thus ours, too) can confer upon it an extraordinary potency. In the scene that initiates the poisoning sequence in *Notorious* we see Claude Rains and Ingrid Bergman at breakfast. The camera pans from a medium shot of him along the table to a medium shot of her, but it departs from the expected geometry of such a straightforward pan. In a combination of tilt and zoom the camera dips to take in Bergman's coffee cup before continuing on its way, and the inexplicable obeisance of the lens (why should an ordinary cup receive such deference?) alerts us to the fact that there is more here than meets the eye. An even more dramatic example from the same film would be the famous crane shot which zooms without a cut from an encompassing view of a crowded entrance hall to a key hidden in Bergman's hand, a visual movement that breaks with cinematic etiquette by ignoring the order of precedence we naturally assign to it. It should do the decent thing and end on Bergman's head and shoulders (roughly centred in the frame as we approach) but it cuts her, descending instead to her hand and conceding all the narrative power of the scene to that tiny object.

Close-ups also take advantage of the fact that we attribute to large objects qualities of inertia and weight – we obey the general equivalence between size and mass that the world has taught us. In *Tirez sur le Pianiste*, when Charles Aznavour hesitates before pressing the bell of the concert agent who will transform his career, the extreme close-up of his finger hovering over the button gives genuine weight to the moment of decision, a suggestion both of inertia to be overcome and the vastness of this decision. And the sense that the physics of large objects always colours our inspection of enlargements onscreen is further underlined by the simple practical fact that slow motion will often have to be employed to keep moving close-ups within the frame for long enough to be seen (without it, after all, they would arrive and depart with comical abruptness). The pool balls in Scorsese's *The Color of Money* move with the ponderous gravity of planets, as if the weight of everything that orbited around them – money, happiness, pride – had been concentrated within their shining surfaces. You almost expect them to rumble as they roll, an aural confirmation of their crushing power. And sometimes this invocation of the physical obedience of objects, their dependable subjection to laws that apply outside the cinema, has a peculiarly literal force. What is the most massive image in *Jurassic Park*, a film successfully sold on the promise of immensity? I would argue that it is the tiny ripples we are shown in a plastic beaker of water, a seismic register of terrible approaching mass.

But there can also be a kind of weightlessness to the extreme close-up – a sense that when objects are detached from their implication in the world they float free, ready to absorb whatever meanings we wish to attach to them. The more 'poetic' a close-up, in the sense of being detached from the prosaic purposes of the film, the more we are returned to a kind of delirium of seeing, in which magnification becomes less an analytical dissection of its qualities than an opportunity to revel in what it can be made to mean. In *Three Colours: Blue*, Krzysztof Kieślowski begins his tale of bereavement with an extreme close-up of a fragment of blue paper held by a child's hand out of a car window. The image itself is initially ambiguous – it isn't easy to say what this flickering blue object is – and it has no evident purpose in the sequence in which it appears, a set of shots showing a car speeding along a road. We can relish the sheen of light on its surfaces (close-ups are exceptionally good at restoring the lustre of the world, otherwise dimmed by our inattention) and we can ascribe meanings to it – an intimation of fragility or tinsel flimsiness, the innocence of a child's vision – but they remain fugitive, snatched away just as the paper itself is finally snatched away by the wind. Unlike other images in Kieślowski's films, which dazzle for a time but seem later to be revealed as a kind of fraud upon the viewer (the nocturnal swimming pool in *Three Colours: Blue*, for example, open all hours to serve as a shallow symbol of respite), this holds its mystery, flickering between portent and mere appearance so rapidly that we cannot ever quite fix its nature.

Eisenstein (or his translator) described in *Film Form* this capacity to isolate objects from their connections to the mundane world as an 'abstraction of the lifelike', and his phrase recurs in another passage that speaks vividly to this sense of the transcendent experience of the close-up. In one of his aphorisms on aesthetics, Schopenhauer talks of perceiving the Platonic idea of an object:

> The perception of this, however, demands that, when contemplating an object, I really abstract its position in space and time, and thus abstract its individuality. For it is this position, always determined by the law of causality, which places this object in any kind of relationship to me as an individual; so that only when this position is done away with will the object become an *Idea*.*

What Schopenhauer effectively describes here is a photographic procedure – an exercise of perception that can rescue elements of the world from its restrictive implications. His description of a kind of transcendent contemplation might be taken as a rather rarefied way of describing what the cinema has actually made a commonplace experience. If you want to have such Platonic visions these days, you simply need the price of admission (though you will have to choose your film with care if you want the vision to have any durable power).

The cinema camera and the projector are clearly, then, a philosophical machine. But if we want to answer the central

---

Aphorisms on Aesthetics: Essays and Aphorisms, Arthur Schopenhauer, R. J. Hollingdale, Penguin, 1973.

question put earlier, that of what kind of optical instrument the motion picture camera is, then we probably need to go back to another of the scientific instruments on which the great Enlightenment project of vision rested – the camera obscura.

There are obvious connections between the two forms – the dark, enclosed viewing space, the luminous entrapment of a mere portion of the world, the dizzying spectacle of projected movement. Like cinema, the camera obscura presents the world so that it can be admired as a picture. But there are less obvious ones, too. Early accounts of the camera obscura and early descriptions of the experience of cinema are remarkably similar, despite the gap in time between the two technologies, and what unites the two is the perverse conviction that the degraded, mediated spectacle on the wall is somehow more captivating, more authentic, than the original just outside the door. The glaring virtues of cinema repeatedly blind us to its glaring deficiency, its inability to capture more than a fraction of the detail available to our naked eyes. Like the camera obscura, it needs to take refuge in darkened rooms before it can pretend to brilliance – but that flight into protective segregation is also the clue to its power – its freedom from Schopenhauer's 'laws of causality'. The camera obscura could never retie those severed connections (and was, in truth, chained to its surroundings in a way that cinema is not). Cinema, through editing, can, and in that fact lies its extraordinary ability to remake the world. Those who describe the movie camera as a microscope or a magnifying glass miss the point of its enlargements, which are less about close inspection than about a detached way of seeing. The cinema works to restore an animist universe, in which every object is not merely an aggregate of its physical qualities, but is possessed of its own spirit. In doing that it can restore to audiences the feeling of seeing for the first time, and make primitives of us all.

THE UNSEEN OFFSCREEN

The American cartoonist Charles Addams often uses cinemas as locations for his deadpan dramas of the uncanny – perhaps because those crepuscular spaces provide a perfect rendezvous for the banal and the inexplicable. But he is also an artist with an interest in events that take place outside the frame of the drawing – mysteries or horrors that intrude in some way into the image we are viewing. In one cartoon, for example, a couple in a hotel room are startled from their mundane business by the appearance of a row of knife points that have pierced the party wall, and that neatly outline the figure of a woman. In another drawing a woman shouts frantically up at the sky: 'George, George. Drop the keys!' – and only the shadow of a vast bird with a human figure in its beak reveals to us (a crucial beat or two after reading the caption) what has just taken place. In yet another drawing a crowd of nurses and doctors emerges screaming from a maternity ward, their panic at odds with the mildly quizzical expression on the cat-eyed, puffball-headed figure waiting patiently outside. All three have the displaced centre of attention that is characteristic of many Addams cartoons – and that can give them a quality of deceptive ordinariness on first inspection. And all seem to me essentially cinematic in their operation, because they depend for their effectiveness on something *not* directly observed. These jokes rely on the sense of what has just happened or is just about to; in other words, they propose an imaginary sequence of events from which this is a single, insinuating frame. But they could not do that without exploiting our ability to see beyond our immediate field of vision – to project our own pictures into the blank spaces of the image.

'There is in every film a region of shadow, a stockpile of the not seen,' notes the French screenwriter Jean-Claude Carrière in *The Secret Language of Film*. It is a useful reminder of how much there is in a cinema image that will never physically strike our retinas. One might want to reverse the terms of his cartography, however. It would be as true to say that all films are a small region of light in a continent of the not seen, and in this chapter I want to consider how cinema learnt to enter and exploit that territory. In doing so it did not merely enlarge its sphere of operations; it transformed itself from a spectacular novelty into an art form, one possessed of the essential artistic capacity to make implications. The narrative is not just one of imperial expansion – a desire to push beyond the limiting geometry of a small rectangular screen – but one of liberation. In emancipating itself from the visible this youthful medium achieved its true maturity.

The most pertinent of Addams's cartoons in this respect is the one in which a cinema auditorium is shown from the back of the theatre. The cinema is full and the image on the screen is of a young woman adopting one of cinema's more familiar iconographic poses – The Apprehension of Immediate Danger. Her hands are raised to either side of her face, and her mouth and eyes are wide open in terror. Her eye line is aimed directly at you and the punchline of the joke (which has no punchline since it is, in an unusually literal sense, a sight gag) is that her gaze is echoed by every member of the audience. Row after row of anxious faces have swivelled round to see what it is that has so terrified the actress on screen. There are several reasons why this cartoon is funny – or at least why its essentially simple joke will survive some extended looking. It is a nice detail, for instance, that the expressions on the faces in the audience are not terrified but timorous and uncertain. The starlet on screen knows exactly what it is that she is reacting to but these people are still in doubt. It is as if at some level they know there is nothing to fear, but that rictus onscreen has *compelled* them to turn. This being a Charles Addams cartoon, there is also an uneasy ambiguity to the image. After all, it may not be a joke about cinematic convention at all; perhaps something really *has* entered the cinema outside *our* field of vision and this is an eerie coincidence we are witnessing, in which a horror designed for entertainment has perfectly synchronized itself with a more substantial threat.

It also matters to the effect of the thing that the audience so solidly middle aged in appearance. The joke would not be funny if the audience was composed of children, partly because childish anxiety isn't as secure an object of humour, but also because it would be far more plausible that children might not fully understand the convention of the reaction shot – the unwritten promise that if we are patient the camera will eventually show us what is being looked at with such intensity of emotion. Similarly, if Addams had resorted to those other members of his cartoon stock company – primitive tribesmen – the joke would have been diminished to the point of non-existence. In either case there would have been something faintly condescending about the cartoon, as if it mocked a perfectly blameless innocence. As it is, what we see is a derailment of expectation as unsettling as that produced by the famous Addams cartoon in which a skier's tracks trace an impossible route either side of a tree trunk. What would the experience of film be like if audiences *genuinely* believed that the world onscreen projected out into the one they comfortably occupy?

But that audiences do believe in such reciprocal projection, at some level, hardly needs saying. Indeed, it is difficult to believe that cinema, as we know it now, would even be possible without our propensity to extrapolate from the limited information onscreen, to build an extended space that overlaps in strange ways with the physical space we occupy as we watch the film. As the Addams cartoon reminds us, the unseen and the offscreen are inseparable from our sense of involvement in the stories cinema tells – the feeling that we have, in some way, become incorporated in the world they depict. It also reminds us that special rules apply to this imaginary space: it is a place in which we cannot be touched (which is why the terror is bearable), but also a place in which we are powerless to be vigilant on our own behalf (which is one of the reasons we feel the fear personally, rather than vicariously, in sympathy with those on screen). For the director of a thriller or a horror movie the manipulation of these qualities is likely to be a specialized skill, applied with nice calculation. But all film is dependent, to some greater or lesser degree, on what we cannot see. Cinema is made possible as an art form by our blindness as well as our vision.

There is a rather obvious sense in which this is true: a film in its making consists of countless scenes that can never be witnessed if the illusion of the film is to be maintained, from the untidy sprawl of equipment and technicians that surround the action to the alternative takes and rehearsals that make a scene possible. When this pretended absence is exposed – as when a sound boom dips below the upper border of the screen – the result is a passing moment of deflation, as if that penetrating object has pierced a barrier between our world and that of the film. We may even feel a momentary contempt for the film, which derives less from the fact that a professional task has been flunked than because we can suddenly see through the fiction to the machinery of its creation. If the integrity of the fictional envelope is maintained, on the other hand, film can easily blur the distinction between accidents and intention. However sharp our vision, the image onscreen may contain meanings that we cannot see. Sheldon Kahn, the editor *of One Flew over the Cuckoo's Nest*, recalls how, during shooting, Louise Fletcher – who plays the disapproving Nurse Ratchet – had been filmed while preparing for a scene.

She sort of sniffed and reacted to what Milos had said because she was registering it in her mind at that point. I noticed that particular attitude as a wonderful reaction to be used somewhere in the picture. When I was cutting the scene in which Jack Nicholson comes back from electroshock treatment where he's walking stiff like Frankenstein, one of the cuts I went to was Louise Fletcher doing her sniff and giving a sideways glance... It was a wonderful reaction of her seeing him after his 'treatment'*

Martin Scorsese tells a very similar story about the filming of a scene in *Raging Bull*, in which Jake La Motta accuses his brother of having an affair with his wife: 'I told Bob I wasn't getting enough reaction from Joe Pesci. He told me to roll the camera again, and then said, "Did you fuck your mother?" When you see the film again, look at Joe's reaction!'† This invitation to the interviewer to look again perfectly captures the paradox of cinematic candour – a pretence of openness and revelation that is made up of countless concealments. Viewed in the light of this anecdote, the scene contains a sight that was previously invisible, though the image has undergone no physical change; what's more, without our blindness to that local truth about the origin of Pesci's expression we would be unable to see the constructed truth of that moment in the film. (Indeed, once you know the anecdote that particular sequence in the film becomes impossible ever to watch in quite the same way again. The knowledge that there is a shard of authentic and ungoverned feeling embedded in the scene's dissimulation makes your inspection alert and archaeological; you find yourself looking for the fragment in a way that inevitably renders the whole more obscure.)

From the first occasion on which Georges Méliès used the secret spaces offered by editing to make a man disappear before your eyes (secret because he did the best he could to make all traces of the edit disappear as well), this kind of sleight of hand has been essential to cinema – that is, both of its essence and

---

First Cut: Conversations with Film Editors, University of California Press.
†*Scorsese on Scorsese*, ed. Ian Christie, Faber, London, 1997.

Film buffs will almost certainly be able to add to this brief account of cinematic opportunism. A variation on the theme is supplied by the scene in *Gone with the Wind* in which Clark Gable celebrates the birth of his first child with Scarlett, by toasting the birth with Hattie McDaniels. The actors were supposed to drink tea to represent the sherry of the storyline, but Gable secretly substituted whiskey. Victor Fleming enjoyed the surprised grin McDaniels produced enough to include it in the final cut.

indispensable to it. It seems appropriate, somehow, that the verb 'to screen' should have meant to conceal or hide something before it came to mean showing a film, because the dead ground out of our eye line is precisely where the foundation stones of cinematic meaning are laid.

I used the word 'obvious' about the concealment of a film's processes. But it's probably worthwhile to recall the etymology of 'obviousness', which derives from the Latin *obviam*. The obvious is both what is unmissable and what is 'in the way' or across our path. It may be a barrier to understanding as much as its simple object. When we think of those fabled audience members who ran from the screenings of the Lumière brothers' *L'Arrivée d'un Train à La Ciotat* (audience members whose admirable imaginative commitment to cinema was almost immediately mocked in comic films), we may think that the explanation of their alarm is self-evident. Their biological skill at extrapolation told them the train was on a collision course with the left-hand wall of the auditorium. It was simple common sense to get out of the way. Lacking experience in cinematic projection, they took it, momentarily no doubt, for an original not a recording. But how was it that the self-evident unreality of that image – its eerie absence of colour, its unnerving, gauzy rendering, the unearthly silence – should be overcome by the limited novelty of its realism? How was it possible for anyone to be so possessed by the moving image that they yielded up their own sense of the world so completely?

The answer can only lie in the unprecedented vividness of what lay within that lighted rectangle, a sight so startling that it effectively erased everything that surrounded it. The literalism of the cinema image loomed very large as its principal charm – so large, indeed, that it effectively obscured its greater potential. The veracity of cinema's record of the physical world was, as many early accounts testify, a saving grace for spectators who were ill at ease in the presence of this faintly disreputable novelty, a clattering nonsense that seemed (and, for a time, was) absolutely at odds with any aesthetic principle. The startling

verisimilitude of the depiction, its contingent, superfluous rendering of details, appeased even those audience members who
found the antics on display callow or vulgar.* As well as being
its principle wonder, though, the very superfluity of the cinematic image was prima-facie evidence of its lack of artistry, its
absence of discriminating intelligence. Excluding nothing that
was placed in front of it, the camera constantly betrayed its
mechanical lack of judgement – that human ability to select
and, by selecting, to reduce the banal plenitude of the world
into a comprehensible meaning. In its infancy, cinema was so
infatuated by what could be shown in a new way that it could
spare no attention at all for what lay untouched all around it:
the imagined space just outside the screen where it would find
the means by which it could become an art.

The history of the medium won't offer any simple trajectory
of learning along which audiences proceed – becoming progress-
ively more sophisticated about the conventions on which their
pleasure depends. As *L'Arrivée d'un Train à La Ciotat* demonstrated, the unseen space implied by a cinema image
(particularly a documentary image) is not some late refinement
of the cinematic experience; it is there from the very start,

---

*It is possible to wonder whether the history of cinema might have been different
had the medium been developed at a time when the dominant cultural principle
was something other than truth to life (Realism was at the end of its imperial
sway, but had not yet been displaced). One might put this question another way
and ask whether, in that alternative universe, cinema could have been considered
as anything but a prodigiously useful perceptual instrument. There are, after all,
many technologically innovative forms of recording an image that have not
generated a cultural industry – microscopy and X-rays, among others. Indeed,
there were those who took it for granted that moving pictures were entirely
functional in their prospects. In the work of Eadweard Muybridge and the
development of his Zoopraxiscope we are naturally inclined to detect the first
germs of the twentieth century's dominant cultural form. He simply saw an
effective tool for studying the locomotion of animals. Maxim Gorky, too, watching
those early Lumière scenes, assumed that the device was practical in its purposes:
'I do not yet see the scientific importance of the Lumières' invention but, no
doubt, it is there, and it could probably be applied to the general ends of science,
that is, of bettering man's life and the developing of his mind' (from a newspaper
article of 4 July 1896, reprinted in *Roger Ebert's Book of Film*, Norton, 1996).

absolutely bound to the initial understanding of cinema as a photographic experience – in other words, a medium that cuts segments from the world rather than *modelling* an alternative one from some pliable medium (whether that be language or wood or clay or theatrical flats). The assumption of a physical continuity between the world onscreen and the one that the viewer occupies is immediate and natural (not naïve, as we are inclined to see it now). There simply was no precedent for the sight of a walking man who disappeared from a proscenium frame *to go nowhere*. On the stage you knew he would be in the wings – in the cinema there had to be some realm too that would admit him. And without that innate sense of continuity (which has the force of a vital prejudice, biologically hard-wired) it is also difficult to believe that the extreme artifice of edited continuity would ever have been acceptable. For what is involved in showing a man walking from one room to another by means of edits is a violent and instantaneous movement of the audience's point of view. At one moment we are in the room and the next out of it, and that our comprehension can survive such wrenches is remarkable. (Prose literature may seem to offer a foretaste of such moves but it doesn't really. It can certainly move a reader with great rapidity from one scene to another but it does not – in the course of a single character's movement – shift with such mercurial and unpredictable darts from one perspective to another. The novel is heavily dependent on the Steadicam.)

There is some evidence in the early days of cinema that this sudden and essentially inexplicable movement from one vantage point to another constituted an embarrassment for the pioneers. What narrative explanation, after all, might you offer for the propensity of the camera to pass instantly through walls or – even more striking – to be simultaneously present in two places? And before this could be properly exploited as part of the delirium of the new medium it had to be accommodated, absorbed or digested by means of devices that softened its sharp perceptual disjunctions. In *Film Style and Technology*, Barry

Salt writes of the increasing popularity of the dissolve in the early 1900s as a means of joining together two disjunctive sequences of film, and he also points out that its current accepted meaning in film vocabulary – as an indication of compressed time – 'did not begin to be established as a convention till the end of the nineteen twenties'. But there was never really a time when the dissolve *didn't* have temporal implications. When Méliès – in *La Voyage dans la Lune* – dissolves from a scene in which visitors are inspecting the spacecraft in a workshop to a scene in which (having mounted a staircase in the first scene) they appear on the roof immediately above, he is easing his audience through the startling immediacy of that cut, giving them time to gather speed and get under way. The dissolve spreads out the cut in time so that its cutting edge is blunted.

Similarly, fade cuts and iris cuts (in which the image shrinks gradually only to expand again on a different sight) now strike us as attempts to solve a conundrum that we no longer have. It would seem likely that such devices (and perhaps even the dissolve, which had clear precedents in certain stage-lighting effects) are essentially theatrical in nature – that they derive from an art form in which time was essential for a change of scenery. More importantly, they derive from an art form in which all change of perspective is essentially static in nature – a succession of locations that are rarely continuous one with another and that we can guarantee will remain stable for some time. And the crucial point is not that cinema is liberated from such tedious furniture shifting – because it takes just as long to relocate the camera – but that it discovers, for the first time, a way to excise the labour from the finished product. This is the magic from which Méliès constructs his early spectacles: that an apparently seamless passage of time can be stitched into an invisible pocket that will conceal the working of a trick.

For Méliès, cinema appeared to start and stop with such conjuring – he regarded the story as 'a mere thread to link the "effects" ' – and it is odd that so much time elapses before this example of what could be done is applied to more coherent kinds of narrative. The development of continuity cutting has the feel of an evolutionary, even an inadvertent discovery. It coalesced slowly, as if brought into being by a series of accidents, and impatience was among the evolutionary pressures. Several distributors were in the habit of cutting out the time-consuming iris ins and outs, and discovered that when they did so the audience was quite capable of surviving the perceptual jolt. 'Cut to the chase' – that cinematic expression of frustrated urgency – is a phrase that neatly encapsulates both the invention and its inspiration. (It was some time before film-makers discovered that it wasn't actually necessary either to give the audience time to adjust to its new surroundings, to 'get its eye in', as it were. Until then, cuts would often include a redundancy that appears bizarre to contemporary audiences, so that you would see a complete sequence of a man leaving the room, followed by a complete sequence of him entering the next one, a cut that inevitably doubled up on some of his actions). And what is intriguing here – as cinema slowly constructs a grammar that will effectively serve it for another hundred years – is that innovation is bent not towards what the audience can see but what they can't or don't need to. It is only when cinema discovers how little it needs to show that it can begin to grow in sophistication.

Continuity cutting emerges because of the desire to expand the boundaries of a space that is otherwise claustrophobically fixed, both because of the static nature of early cameras and the theatrical model on which many 'views' (the French term for a short film) are based. But the realization that a number of static one-directional views could successfully be assembled into an elaboration of three-dimensional space brings the invisible space around the camera into play in a way that would not otherwise have been likely. When a cinema screen was still an imaginary proscenium arch, offscreen was virtually indistinguishable from offstage – a kind of limbo in which characters can be held until needed. But what is out of sight beyond the borders of the screen soon comes to have a positive potential rather than serve merely as a vacancy into which images depart. The theatre audience knows that offstage is permanently inaccessible to it. Even if a director plays games of revelation, with a revolve stage or some other device, there remains a space beyond the theatrical arena that cannot be reached, a range of sights that we can be confident we will not be shown. Our own physical inertia, seated as we are inside four walls, serves as a guarantor that what is immediately in front of us will take precedence over the imagined space elsewhere. But no such conviction attaches to offscreen space, which, whether it is the other side of the door or the other side of a mountain range, is immanent at all times. Imminent too – given that cuts do not need to announce themselves in advance. The feeling of claustrophobia that is often detected when theatrical hits are adapted for the screen derives from this distinction – between an art form that has to find reasons to stay in one place and one that barely needs reasons to be always elsewhere.

Directors soon learnt to colonize this unfound land, penetrating the border between what is seen and what is not. It wasn't long before they were bending the unyielding geometry of the screen in ways that allowed your imagination to turn corners that light cannot. When Cecil B. DeMille makes the bars of a prison cell cast their shadow on a character, you are effectively looking at the projection of a projection, the essential technology of cinema turned at a right angle imaginatively to extend the space sideways. DeMille was fond of this device, particularly to alert the audience to the presence of a villain before he actually enters the frame (his use of a shadow that falls like a sentence of death across a sleeping figure predates that in *Nosferatu* by several years). Why are these moments so gripping to us? What pleasure do they give us that is not offered by simple cross-cutting to show that danger has entered the room? The answer is only partly to do with the delicious interlude between suspicion and confirmation; it is also important that such devices offer the audience an exercise of alertness, and this operates not just in relation to the insensate character onscreen (so agonizingly unconscious of their proximity to danger) but with regard to the film itself. We like to feel that we have noticed something in advance, that the camera – in some paradoxical way – is less vigilant than we are, because it has not yet thought to turn its own gaze to match our apprehensions.*

Something similar happens in D.W. Griffith's *The Musketeers of Pig Alley*, when the arrival of a character is announced by a gust of cigar smoke, a vaporous intrusion that makes it clear that off-camera space is as potent as that which we can see. Griffith began his cinema career as an actor, working for Edwin S. Porter, the entrepreneur and inventor who made some of the earliest ventures into narrative editing. When Griffith played the lead in Porter's *Rescued from an Eagle's Nest*, he was actually obscured by the edge of the frame, so casual was the set-up. But Griffith as a director soon discovered that to go over the edge is not just to disappear into nothingness; it is to move to that fertile area of a film's field of depiction in which the concrete and the literal give way to poetry and suggestion. What is so powerful about that admonitory gust of cigar smoke – and the countless cinematic annunciations that followed it – is that we are given the pleasure of keen-sightedness in such a way that the most myopic member of the audience could not miss it, the pleasures of deduction in a manner that is accessible to the dimmest mind. Griffith had discovered a way to make

*The soundtrack is partly effective, of course, at alerting us to the presence of danger while the image can remain ostensibly unaware – indeed, music often seems to serve as a kind of switch, flicking our sensibilities from a condition in which they are complacently indifferent to what lies beyond the screen's borders to one in which we can barely think of anything else. Offscreen space has this curious quality, in terms of its aesthetic presence, of flickering from insistence to reticence, and it is not always an easy task to find out how the director has made the connection that switches it on again. There are crude ways of restoring the power, such as a terrified look that has no obvious onscreen object, but far more often the transition occurs with no obvious announcement; the arena in which your imagination must operate suddenly expands beyond the edge of the screen.

the audience act as collaborators in the unrolling story. This factitious flattery of the audience – the pretence that it knows more than the characters onscreen – is still an active pleasure in the cinema. Think of the numerous scenes in which we discover that a character has been under observation, because a figure moves into the extreme foreground of the shot, a presence undetected by anyone in the frame. Think, too, of those occasions when the space *behind* the lens is suddenly animated by an obscuring object immediately in front of it. In *Citizen Kane*, one of the snatched newsreels of Kane as a frail old man is given the authenticating touch of wire-fencing in the near foreground. This is partly a way for Welles to brand the footage as distinct from the unimpeded gaze of classic Hollywood style, but it is also a way of pushing the camera itself forward, out of its habitual hiding into a perceptual space where we cannot help but notice it.*

It is scarcely a collaboration of equals, however. For, at the same time as it discovers the potency of the unseen, cinema discovers another equally crucial attribute of its aesthetic effect: that it has the power to control the vision of its audience to a degree hitherto unthinkable and that this control is as much to do with the withholding of a sight as with its presentation. In a cinema we have our vision both sharpened and dulled. We see things more clearly, but it is tunnel vision too – a disability that can exclude all sense of surrounding context. And every

---

*For similar reasons, bushes or foliage or any masking object very close to the lens have become a readily understood cliché for surreptitious surveillance, a vivid way of making the camera into a malevolent actor in the scene – rather than a recording presence that is notionally altogether absent from the imagined universe of the film. If your film is about the act of filming then it becomes particularly crucial to find some visible badge that will distinguish the guileless gaze from the furtive one. 'The fundamental situation that we had to face was that all movies are shot with concealed cameras, so that in a sense there was no way that you could convey the idea that Truman was being filmed under surveillence,' said Peter Weir, explaining why certain shots in *The Truman Show* had been accented with distortion or intervening clutter – many of which served to establish the location of the camera, as in a recurring shot through the reversed green numerals of a car radio display.

film also constitutes either a rape or a seduction of our normal vision. In the cinema, far more than in an art gallery or a theatre, we temporarily submit our eyes to someone else's command.

Two films strike me as illuminating in this respect. Both of them are popular thrillers, and both of them generate much of their terror through a derangement of sight. In David Cronenberg's *The Dead Zone* and Irvin Kershner's *Eyes of Laura Mars*, the chief motors of the plots are the unwilling visions of the principal characters. Both have been cursed with second sight – the power to foresee tragic or violent events – and for both characters the visions are uncontrollable. The revelations replace their commonplace perceptions of what is around them without warning and cannot then be switched off or dispelled. For the duration of their visions they are, to all intents and purposes, blinded by the terrible cinemas inside their heads. And the audience, seeing exactly what they see as they are seized by premonition, is in a similar plight. It's true that we arrive in the cinema voluntarily, and that we are there for reasons of pleasure. But there is some kinship still between our pleasure and their fate, between our surrender to another person's vision and their unwilling seizures. Like them, we experience a disconnection between the evidence of our eyes and the evidence of our bodies (our eyes tell us we are moving even as our bodies report that we are sitting still). It's true that we can cover our eyes at moments of horror (a kind of protective blindness that no account of the thriller genre should leave out), but nonetheless these visions offer a model for the experience of cinema – its abrupt and sometimes shocking substitution for what we might expect to find in front of our eyes, its aggressive discontinuities.

In *Eyes of Laura Mars*, the cinematic effect is further emphasized by the fact that her visions are point-of-view renderings of what the serial killer sees as he tracks his prey (the fact that this plot is nonsense, incidentally, doesn't detract from the impact of the device). In the film these sequences are presented as a kind of low-quality video, the better to distinguish them from the crisp normality of the camera's vision – a stylistic overlay that seems to argue a distinction between this degraded vision and the hallowed clarity of cinema, but that also reminds you of the camera's power to replace your vision with that of another. In the most powerfully unnerving enlistment of this device, Mars finds herself being chased by the killer, her flight impeded and her terror hugely amplified by the fact that all she can see is the sight of her own retreating back. She watches her flight as her own predator – as we are obliged to watch it too.

This is, incidentally, one of the few uses of extended point-of-view camerawork that doesn't feel actively embarrassing, because it exploits the very disability of that technique: the fact that it will eventually generate in an audience a sense of powerlessness. In a sequence constructed from conventional shots we enjoy a supremacy of vision that elevates us above any single character. In true point-of-view sequences, however, in which the camera does not merely accompany a moving figure but actually stands in for him or her, the audience suddenly finds itself in the imaginary space of the screen as a disadvantaged actor, rather than a privileged observer. This device deprives us of one of the most important pleasures cinema can give us (though it is often the least conscious): that of being invisible ourselves, erased from view by the darkness of the room we sit in and by the fact that we can inspect without ever being inspected. Even worse, we enjoy no enlargement of power to make up for this loss of privilege. Characters onscreen address us directly, but the fact that their eye line demands a response generates an anxiety about the fact that we cannot take action, that we have to wait for that invisible surrogate onscreen to perform for us.

The most sustained example of how uncomfortable this can be is offered by Robert Montgomery's *The Lady in the Lake*, in which what you see is exactly what is seen by the protagonist – who thus appears himself only in reflections. It's arguable, I suppose, that the discomfort the film arouses is in keeping with its artistic ambitions – that film noir is always interested in events running out of control. But when the face of the female lead, Audrey Totter, looms amorously towards the screen, what you feel is a sense of disappointment rather than seductive involvement; the effect is a deflating reminder of your paralysis as a viewer, your frustrated excitement. 'YOU accept an invitation to a blonde's apartment!' declared the promotional blurb. Once there, unfortunately there was nothing you could do to take advantage of your admission.*

In *Eyes of Laura Mars* (and, to a lesser extent, in *The Dead Zone*), this crippling disadvantage is entirely in keeping with what you *should* be feeling – the terror of seeing events that you are powerless to alter, that you can only helplessly watch unwinding. There are, of course, many films in which the tracking shot offers precisely that: a predatory pursuit that combines in the viewer both an apprehension of the vulnerability of the tracked and a sense of panic at the inexorable nature of that movement, which will not respond to your desires. In *Halloween*, for example, John Carpenter is at pains to make clear the connection between the smooth, slow motions of his Steadicam shots and the point of view of his human monster. The opening sequence that establishes this equivalence does fall prey to some of the awkwardnesses that are always attendant on point-of-view shots – such as the fact that whenever an object is picked up it must be held up unnaturally in front of the camera's gaze so that we can see what it is – but like *Eyes of Laura Mars* (for which John Carpenter wrote the script) it turns the disability to good effect. One of the faintly unnerving qualities of point of view is that we cannot see what

*Point of view is the natural choice of format for screen fictions in which the viewer really does have choices about what the protagonist does next – namely role-playing computer games. But it is intriguing to note that some of the most successful continue to use a detached viewpoint, in which the notional camera hovers behind the 'actor'. This is partly due to technological limitations – realistic point of view would narrow the field of vision and, in the absence of a mechanism for easily turning the character's head, the game might be too difficult to play. But I wonder, too, whether a vestigial cinematic nostalgia also governs such decisions.

we are being asked to identify ourselves with – in this case a psychopathic child who murders his sister with a kitchen knife. For the rest of the film, that opening uncertainty affects virtually every tracking or Steadicam shot you see, colouring its smoothness with malign intent. It's a nice detail that the 'inhumanity' of the killer is reinforced by the transparent inhumanity of his movement – eerily unperturbed motions that are the product of hydraulic damping and counterweights, not maniacal determination.

There is another quality of point of view that is relevant here, too, and that is the way it is often inseparable from a sense of restricted or limited vision. In contrast to the master shot, point of view is all subjection. It is forced to move through space to open up new vistas, and each movement forcibly reminds you of how we can look in only one direction at a time (a disability that isn't entirely erased by cinema's ability to cut instantly from one place to another, but that is certainly diminished by it). But in this, point of view only foregrounds what is true of all cinema shots: that the border of the frame does not mark a point at which the imaginary space ceases, just the point at which it falls out of sight. There are cinematic compositions in which an awareness of what lies outside the frame barely impinges, in which neither the eye nor the mind strays away from the centre of the screen, but even there the space remains live, accessible to the director at a moment's notice.

Halloween makes a useful case study for such matters, partly because the creation of cinematic tension is peculiarly dependent on not letting the audience see too much too soon, but also because of the effective vacuity of its plot – a vacancy you can take as pure or trashy according to your disposition. *Halloween* is a film about nothing but how efficiently celluloid can scare you. Carpenter's choice of a suburban idyll as a site for atrocity, the apple-pie domesticity of his setting, means that he must draw on technique rather than objects. And although his film contains several stock Gothic effects – an uprooted gravestone, a stormy night peopled by madmen in night-shirts, a bloodstained knife-blade – it does not really rely on the conventional emblems of horror. Even the monster's face is the white, expressionless blank of a carnival mask – inscrutable and, for large portions of the film, invisible – either because it is just too distant to make out clearly or because Carpenter makes it teasingly skirt the frame.* Instead, he must create his terror out of an amalgam of imaginative projection on our part (our feelings of what would it be like to be in that position, fleeing from such a thing) and our perceptual vulnerability to ambush, which acts as a kind of correlative to the bodily dangers depicted onscreen. We aren't going to get a kitchen knife through the chest, as those frantic, callow, sarcastic (and punishably cupidinous) teenagers will – but there *is* a piercing quality to the sudden dart of adrenalin that follows an unexpected eruption onscreen.

Carpenter has talked about the way in which he closed the frame around his characters, in order to trap them in a space where their ability to see what was coming was greatly diminished, and there are occasions in which you can see the operation of this machinery with particular clarity. Near the beginning of the film, Jamie Lee Curtis is asked by her estate agent father to drop off a set of keys at the Myers house – the location for the murder that initiates the plot and now a place of superstitious dread for the local children. Curtis encounters the young boy she will later baby-sit, who watches uneasily as she walks to the porch, and in the scene that follows Carpenter cuts between a long shot of the house viewed from across the street to a medium close-up filmed from the interior through the mesh frame of the door. It is a rapid alteration of relief and tension, with the long shot reassuring you that nothing is likely to happen quite yet. (Long shots are less compatible with immediate fears, because our field of vision is too expansive and

---

*This is not entirely an invention, of course. From *Nosferatu* onwards the absence of human expression has been a dependable source of panic. It removes from us one of our principle tools of self-preservation – the ability to read emotions in strangers' faces. It is another example, I suppose, of the invisible as a realm in which alarm can easily grow.

controlling to allow a sense of panic to develop. The essential proximity of danger is missing.) Meanwhile, the medium close-up tells you not to be so sure. Whereas the long shot places Curtis at the centre of the frame, securely distant from the screen edge, the reverse angle brings the potential victim within touching distance, both because she is much closer to the imaginary front border of the space (that is, the plane that the screen would occupy if we thought of it as a window giving on to the scene) and because a broad margin of black shadows encroaches hazardously on all sides. When seen from this position her flippancy about the danger looks to be tempting fate, to say the least. If we feel we could reach out and touch her, then someone else might too. And, sure enough, as she retreats, the menacing breathing we have heard on the soundtrack resolves itself into the profile of a watching figure, which emerges from the blackness on the right-hand side. The effect is as if the shadow has bodied forth towards the space she occupied onscreen.

This scene, I would suggest, is not one of those that will make nervous viewers opt for elective blindness and hide their eyes behind their hands. For one thing, it is simply too early in the film for the lead character to be attacked – we can feel fairly confident that Carpenter is only playing with us for the moment, biding his time just as that menacing silhouette appears to be. For another, Lee Curtis's escape route is too open and too easily at hand – she has everywhere to run. That ominous darkness entirely surrounds her but it is separated from her by a screen door, so that anything that emerges from it will not immediately be able to seize her. Much later in the film there is a far more claustrophobic reprise of this moment. After Lee Curtis has discovered her murdered friends in an upstairs bedroom, she slumps back against the door, the frame of which encloses a rectangle of deep shadow to which she has turned her back. As she obeys the distressed heroine's first imperative in a horror movie (Stand Still So The Beast Can Catch Up), a pallid face swims into view beyond her shoulder, appearing with the eerie

graduation of a developing photograph (a fine demonstration
from Carpenter that there can be other ways of distressing the
audience than by simply shouting boo).

Halloween is full of such moments, when the imminence of
attack becomes clear by insinuation, most notably when one
of the victims takes refuge in her car and leans forward, puzzled,
to find the interior of her windscreen fogged with condensation.
We grasp the implication of this fact a split second before the
killer grasps her: it has formed because he has been hiding in
the back of the car and his breath renders its windows opaque,
so that the resulting death struggle can only be dimly glimpsed
through the misted windows. Occasionally, that frosted opacity
is swiped by a scrabbling hand – a calligraphy for the terror we
can't quite discern inside the car.

What Carpenter exploited so effectively here and elsewhere
in *Halloween* was the audience's need for a blank screen for
their own mental projections, a space within that busy image
where their own imaginations might operate. 'In my opinion,'
Alfred Hitchcock once said, 'the chief requisite for an actor is
the ability to do nothing well, which is by no means as easy as
it sounds.'* What he meant was that it was the actor's task to
offer a physiognomic canvas that the director and audience
could fill in according to their own desires. Granted this is an
unusual application of the principle. Classically the vacancy has
been supplied within the frame by darkness – shadow being
one of the film director's most potent stimulants. Orson Welles
famously converted darkness into opulence in some of the
Xanadu interiors for *Citizen Kane*, forced by the exigencies of
his budget to press-gang the audience as set decorators. Most
of them prove up to the task, happily furnishing the wedges of
blackness in Welles's images with an extravagant splendour that
has as its seed a single well-lit object. Nor was set-dressing the
limit of the audience's abilities; the instinctive abhorrence of

Hitchcock: Interviewed by François Truffaut, Simon and Schuster, New York,
1985.

the human animal for a visual vacuum could be exploited in all kinds of ways to supply what the film could not. The point is well made in a scene from *The Bad and the Beautiful*, Vincente Minnelli's satire on Hollywood manners. Kirk Douglas and a colleague are attempting to come up with a suitable costume for the cat people in their low-budget thriller. Actors in cat suits have already been dismissed as risible, but the budget will clearly not allow for anything much more elaborate. Then Douglas has a brain wave: 'What scares the human race more than any other single thing?' he excitedly asks his colleague. 'The dark . . .' comes the reply. 'Of course . . . and why? Because the dark has a life of its own. In the dark things come alive.' This makes the point well enough, but is subtly awry as far as cinematic dark is concerned. The cinematic dark does not have a life of its own – not, at least, in the sense that it is inhabited by autonomous objects or threats. In truth, it only has the life that we confer upon it, encouraged by the careful insinuations of the director.*

That scene in *The Bad and the Beautiful* is clearly an allusion to Jacques Tourneur's *Cat People*, a sparely inventive horror movie that depends almost entirely on absences and implications for its effect. Tourneur knew that the audience's imaginations were accessible to him only in proportion to the space left for them to operate, and his cinematic dictum – 'The less you see, the more you believe' – economically captures the essential principle. Show the monster and the audience will be able to look nowhere else; don't show it and the audience are liable to see it everywhere – in the movement of leaves, in the sudden flicker of light reflected off water, in the fluttering breath

*It doesn't have to be darkness, incidentally, even if cultural tradition, economy and ease of set-up are all prejudiced in its favour. The final scene of *Close Encounters of the Third Kind* offers an instance of brilliant light being used for the same effect: to unsight us sufficiently that our imaginations will make good the deficiencies of the costume design. And though the effect of the light here is manifestly benign – drawing on a religiose symbolism with which the audience would be familiar – there are also films in which malevolence lurks, half-glimpsed, at the heart of a dazzling effulgence.

125

of a frightened woman. And Tourneur uses the limitations of our field of vision in a particularly playful way, as in the scene in which Jane Randolph, who plays a work colleague of the mysterious Irena's husband, is stalked by some unseen presence in a lonely street. The passage ends with the hissing pounce of a bus, entering suddenly from screen left. Jane Randolph jumps, though it is almost inconceivable that her perception, untrammelled by any blinkering frame, could be as narrow as ours. Indeed, one of the reasons that the psychology of characters in horror movies can appear so reckless to us, to diverge so grossly from common sense, is because, as paradoxical as it might sound, we forget that the people onscreen are not in a movie, while we are, imaginatively projected into a space that offers us no consolations of familiarity. Horror films are often falsely libelled in this respect; we sneer at their risible lack of psychological consistency, forgetting that these hapless victims know nothing of the threat and have a field of vision that doesn't oppress them with the imminence of attack.

For us, the very invisibility of the threat, the fact that it won't hold still to be observed and measured by the mind, adds to its elusive menace. There must be some biological inheritance at work here; film can trigger in us primitive reflexes of flight and yet it places us imaginatively in an environment in which the cues of sight and sound do not operate. We have the terror of a threat sensed but not yet identified, so that our instincts for self-preservation are held in tortured suspension. How can you flee successfully when you have no idea in which direction the danger lies? And to the inherent paralysis of cinema – our hypnotic susceptibility to the dreadful things it wishes to do to us – is added the paralysis of insufficient information. In *Cat People* this had the freshness of an invention – a novelty that transformed the limitations of B-movie film-making into an artistic strength. It wasn't, in truth. Describing a tense scene in *Alexander Nevsky* in his essay 'The Film Sense', Eisenstein notes that 'at this point the enemy is shown only through the Russian army's expectation of it', an earlier recognition that the offscreen space could be made pregnant by an onscreen look. But Tourneur did see that popular film could absorb the sophistication of this grammar, in which a transitive expression is offered for which we have to supply an object.

The durability of the general principle (and its application to the most expensive movies) is well demonstrated by the production history of Spielberg's *Jaws*. According to one account, Spielberg originally intended to reveal his shark during the early scenes of the movie, but horrendous problems with the hydraulics and guidance system of his animatronic stand-in made it impossible for 'Bruce' to perform on call. Studio executives were becoming increasingly impatient to see some concrete evidence that the expensive location shooting was proving worthwhile. At first Spielberg put them off, hoping to solve his special-effects problems, but when it became impossible for him to postpone a screening of rushes any longer, he was obliged to cut together the sequences he *had* filmed without an onscreen monster, at which point it became clear that the threat was far more powerfully alive as a potential than as a reality. As in *Cat People*, the absence of visible danger both amplifies the sense of encroaching threat and enhances an important ambivalence in the plot. In *Cat People* we cannot be sure for some time whether Simone Simon's character is a case study in sexual pathology or might genuinely represent a supernatural rebuke to the rational certainties of Dr Judd, her complacently sceptical psychiatrist. In *Jaws* the absence of incontrovertible evidence for the shark makes it at least more plausible that Roy Scheider's Chief of Police might succumb to the pressure to keep the holiday beaches open (even though the underwater point-of-view camera leaves us in little doubt that his instincts will eventually be proved correct).

It is hard to know whether to believe this account of an accidental origin for the film's most memorable sequences – passages in which a concealed danger can only be conjectured by its superficial effect. (The most memorable of these is the night-time scene in which two amateur fishermen attempt to catch the shark with a baited line attached to the jetty. After the shark has pulled one section of the jetty free, plunging a man into the water, its unseen movements can be tracked by the movement of the wreckage to which it is attached, so the scene ends with the terrifying comedy of a man swimming for his life from a collection of floating timbers.) But if the story *is* true, Spielberg deserves credit for seeing that nothing needed fixing, that those sequences where the shark is only an implication have a purity of anxiety that is not shared by the scenes in which it finally emerges into the light of day – thirty feet of mechanically chomping grey latex.

What's intriguing about *Jaws*, and perhaps what accounts for the unusual purity of its opening hour, is that the elemental terror that drives the plot – the fear of being out of one's depth – also provides a perfect metaphor for the vulnerability of the cinema-goer. *Jaws* brilliantly exploits the uncertainty of being immersed in an alien medium, one that you know contains life but that cannot be securely invigilated. Like the mind of a viewer immersed in Spielberg's story, the body of a swimmer penetrates into a space that he or she cannot properly inspect, and it is from that that our sense of vulnerability derives. This is captured in the film in underwater scenes where the limits of visibility mean that everything inside the frame is converted into a possible site for ambush. Similarly, when the glittering, opaque surface of the sea fills the screen, we know that the shark might appear from any direction – even directly in front of us.

This is, indeed, how the shark appears for what you might call its first head-and-shoulders shot. Roy Scheider is ladling blood and entrails over the side after a long and fruitless day spent waiting for its appearance. The sea, an even blue, occupies two-thirds of the screen with Scheider's head to the extreme right of the frame; cigarette in mouth, he is exchanging discontented banter with Robert Shaw's ludicrous old salt and Richard Dreyfuss's preppie marine biologist. There is a warning in the dynamics of this set-up. The rather conspicuous way in which

Scheider has turned his back on the likely source of threat makes us uneasy to begin with, but then there is the unbalanced nature of Spielberg's composition to consider, too. He appears to have left room for something that isn't there, and the least cerebral viewer will feel the tension of that missing object (by which I mean that a sense of compositional balance does not require a particularly sophisticated vision – it is an aesthetic disequilibrium that even a nine-year-old would respond to, unconsciously). It isn't long before that missing object arrives, swimming up through the first water-smeared intimation into a sudden and shocking definition.

Whereas in many thrillers our lines of defence are drawn up with regard to physical obstacles or safe zones, here there is no guaranteed space (except for those interludes on land, well away from the water's edge). *Jaws*, a film where the invisible laps up against a crowded sunny beach, is frightening not simply because it touches on atavistic fears but because it finds a new way around our learnt ability to withstand the terrors of film. A rather similar trick was pulled off in the first of the *Alien* films – in many respects simply an adept transposition of the haunted-house movie into space.

Alien is full of dark regions from which danger might spring, and it uses that encroaching geometry to the full (even, in one scene, having the threat descend from the top border of the screen, an underused hiding place in most terrestrial movies, where the common ground of attacker and attacked tends to favour left and right). But the passage that remains vividly in most viewers' minds is the one in which a feral foetus explodes from the stomach of John Hurt – a sequence that unquestionably finds a novel way to spring the cinematic jack-in-the-box. The inward huddle of Hurt's anxious crew-mates and the assumed impermeability of the human body contrive to reassure us that the centre of this image, at least, is a safe zone. There are intimations that something dreadful is coming, it's true. Hurt's retching and the strange convulsions of his torso indicate that a crescendo is under way and that it will not climax well. But even so, the emergence of that head is shocking, at least in part, because it penetrates a surface we have complacently assumed to be inviolable in such circumstances. I wouldn't want to play down the bluntly visceral components of this shock, which has a great deal to do with the blood and imagined pain of such an event. But the fact that this scene plays as a reversal of a conventional attack – first the tearing of flesh and then a sudden scurry to the edge of the screen and away – is inseparable from its effect.* Like the scene in Roman Polanski's *Repulsion* in which grasping hands suddenly push out from the flat surface of a wall, this moment puts the audience on notice that no surface is to be taken for granted (and certainly not the surface of the human body – as is confirmed by the later revelation that Ian Holm is, in fact, an android).

I've concentrated so much on horror movies and thrillers because they are the genre in which apprehension – in the sense both of anticipatory dread and a grasping of material fact – is given its purest expression. It is in such stories that cinema can exploit its power to deny us sight for its most unnerving effects. But that is hardly the limit of its possibilities. Cinema's ability to make us look where it wants us to look always carries with it as a corollary the ability to prevent us looking at what it does not want us to see. And without that ability it's hard to imagine that the medium could have developed as an art form at all. Its insinuating power and its literary sophistication depend on the fact that it can, when it wishes, narrow its line of sight to exclude elements of the world it depicts.

But the space outside the frame is not simply an antechamber,

---

*There are less gruesome examples of this sudden revelation that there is more in the centre of the screen than we had assumed. There's a shot in *Citizen Kane* in which Thatcher, Bernstein and Kane are discussing their financial affairs – the window in the background appears to be only about six feet away, but when Kane suddenly appears (he has been hidden behind Bernstein, whose silhouette looms in the foreground) he walks steadily away, revealing that it is actually an enormous window in the distance. It is a teasing play with our expectations that can stand for all of the sleights of hand Welles employs in the film. Welles was, of course, keen on conjuring tricks.

by means of whose creaking floor we are given warning that something evil this way comes. It is also an intermediate space into which the unshowable (for whatever reason) can be secluded without entirely removing it from our imaginative grasp.

In some periods of cinema's history this formal looking away can take on the force of a communicative ceremony. In *The Public Enemy* there's a scene in which James Cagney and Eddie Woods follow their old mentor Putty Nose home with revenge in mind. Fearing they intend to kill him, Putty Nose sits down at the piano, hoping to play on their memories of old singsongs in his dubious youth club (a front for a Fagin-like fencing operation). When the camera turns away from the piano we know, from the decorum of the motion alone, that murder is about to take place. Only an act of violence could account for this grave aversion from the natural gravitational centre of the scene; only murder could account for the dislocation of what is most prominent on the soundtrack (Putty Nose's nervous singing) from what is most prominent in the frame. There is a premonition in this turning aside and it is not properly resolved until the shot rings out and Putty Nose strikes his final dissonant chord, falling forward on the keys.

There are pre-cinematic precedents for this, of course – a long tradition of theatrical narrative in which the extreme and transgressive deed would take place offstage, only to be described later in acceptably appalled terms. But as we've seen already, there is something far more emotionally intimate about what is offscreen than what is offstage, a perpetual sense that only a tiny motion would bring the atrocity back into view. This scene, with its willed refusal to look, is rather different in tone to the scene much later in the film when the climactic shoot-out takes place – Cagney having entered the headquarters of his rivals while the camera remains fixed on the opposite side of the street. There we are likely to feel a charge of dread, as if the camera had lost its nerve and didn't want to expose itself to the fierce odds that Cagney scorns. In the scene of Putty

Nose's murder, on the other hand, the implications are more uneasy, of a half-hearted complicity in the crime we hear taking place. It is not a simple matter to say whether the camera here is solicitous of the audience or a representative of its ambiguous feelings about what it wishes to view.

The Public Enemy begins with playfulness about what it is possible to show on the screen. The principal players introduce themselves, all smiling broadly and accompanying their poses with some small characteristic gesture: Cagney makes a rabbit punch and lifts his eyebrow sardonically, Jean Harlow gives a tiny wink and Eddie Woods wipes his nose with the back of his hands. They all look directly at us in these portrait cameos, and the mood is one of knowing complicity with the audience, so that when a pious title card appears ('It is the ambition of the authors of *The Public Enemy* to honestly depict an environment that exists today in a certain strata of American life, rather than glorify the hoodlum or the criminal') we have already been brought in on the game. What follows, we are assured by these gestures, will not be a sermon, despite that canny acknowledgement of the current moral panic about cinema, which had led to the creation of the Production Code just a year before (although it would not be strictly applied for a another few years). The credit sequence is fair warning of the film's blackly comic inventiveness with regard to casual violence. The scene in which Cagney grinds half a grapefruit into Mae Clarke's face and the film's conclusion, in which Cagney is delivered to his mother's door, wrapped like a macabre present, both have an unnerving edge of absurdity to them, as if the cruelty had been displaced into a murderous slapstick.

But though *The Public Enemy* averts its gaze from time to time, it doesn't substitute anything for the images it shuns. Indeed, it is part of the film's abiding modernity that it leaves us with nothing to look at for so long when Cagney has entered the rival gang's headquarters (not even the sort of camera movement that often accompanies inert images, as a way of mitigating their affront to a paying audience). We have no way of knowing what is happening behind the opaque glass window of that shop front. This suspension of the camera's usual prurience – its insistence on having a front row seat at the dramas it depicts – is an effective mark of dread. In the scene in which Putty Nose is murdered, for instance, it is very difficult to recall what it is the camera frames as the shot rings out; all that matters is that we are steered away from a sight that has been declared unwatchable. (And that the deed happens anyway, even though the camera is not looking, seems to bolster our sense that these events have an existence quite independent of the observer who generates them.)

These days, of course, such deliberate masking of our perception is much rarer. Films are routinely explicit, their visual surfaces unfolded so that there are no concealing pockets in which atrocity can be tucked away. When such moments of decorum occur they usually indicate that a special act of discretion has taken place. In *Seven*, for example, a film that specifically traded on the unflinching gaze, which it turned on decomposition and bodily damage, only the sight of the detective's wife's decapitated head is withheld from us, presumably because our sensibilities – quite capable of relishing morbid lividity and third-degree burns when inflicted on strangers – would demur at turning the same prurient gaze on a beheaded Gwyneth Paltrow. There was a time when the camera's modesty about violent death used to extend to everyone; these days it is only for those who have already won our sympathies.

It's only fair to admit that *Seven* generates a considerable charge of dismay by keeping its distance from that final appalling revelation. After a succession of scenes that have left nothing to the imagination, the film concludes by leaving everything to it. As in *The Public Enemy*, we are obliged to fill the vacancy ourselves, choosing our own level of detail. But decorum need not be so bleak or blank. A year after William Wellman's gangster film, Howard Hawks's *Scarface* was to demonstrate how cunningly ornamented and suggestive a veil could be. When Boris Karloff is killed, the shooting takes place in a bowling alley. You see the ball leave his hand and travel slowly down the alley where it knocks down the pins – for a moment one of them spins unstably, a giddy equilibrium that finally ends with it toppling to join the others. As a form of modesty, this sequence has a witty shamelessness (not to mention a touch of the miraculous – at least one of the things you feel when you see the shot is the near impossibility of making an inanimate object 'die' with such a hammy stagger). The scene obliges the audience to look away from what, at heart, they wish to see, only to console them with a clever metaphor for what is taking place outside their field of vision. For Truffaut, this passage was quintessential cinema, but it's curious that his account of the sequence in *The Films of My Life* suggests that the viewer actually *sees* Karloff's killing. He writes: 'He squats down to throw a ball in a game of ninepins and doesn't get up; a rifle shot prostrates him.' In fact, the gun goes off well after Karloff has passed out of sight. Truffaut's memory appears to have succumbed to the penetrating power of Hawks's cinematic 'shot' – his ingenious visual pun for the fall of a criminal kingpin.*

The scene in *Scarface* is a fine moment of cinema – a moment that reminds us that the literalism of the cinematic image has always contained an element of oppression for an artist. Because of the gratuitous informativeness of the photographic image (which throws in all kinds of details for free), film can some-times only attain its full suggestive force by turning away from the object of its attention. But that scene gives as much as it takes away; it tenders to the audience's appetite for vision in a way that is not our first concern here. Film's ability to make

---

*There may well be a task of Borgesian scholarship to be conducted here: a cataloguing of cinema's imaginary frames – that is, those sights that people will assure you they saw but for which no celluloid evidence can be found when you return to the film itself. Such chimeras were more common before the advent of video, when a faulty memory was often the only screening room available, but they still exist today. Ask a friend if they saw a pair of satanic infant eyes at the end of *Rosemary's Baby* and you may be surprised to find how vivid that non-existent moment is.

a silent poetry has been a conspicuous feature of its virtues for close on a hundred years, and it can always exploit our desire – which amounts almost to a self-fulfilling belief – that something held in the centre of our field of vision must have significance. What is more curious is the way in which a genuine frustration of our desire to look can also provoke insights in us. I have in mind those occasions when a director can tease us by withholding what is visibly within reach – by insisting that he or she controls the regard of the camera, not our curiosity. When, in *Three Colours: Blue*, Kieślowski holds on the face of a hitchhiker as we hear the sound of a car crashing offscreen, the director's frustration of our instinct (to turn at once towards the sound and to act upon it) reminds us that we are only spectators here, and disadvantaged spectators at that.

In *Vivre sa Vie*, Godard films the opening conversation between Nana (Anna Karina) and Paul from behind their backs, depriving us of the ability to read their faces, which might offer an emotional caption to their words. When Karina turns to Paul and asks, 'What does that look mean?', we are, rather literally, in no position to propose an answer, because though Karina's face does appear in shot, tantalizingly blurred in the mirror of the bar in which they are sitting, Paul's reflection is obscured by the back of her head.

Such moments hover oddly between humility and arrogance, between an acknowledgement of the limitations of the cinematic frame (its permanent estrangement from three-dimensional life) and a perverse excitement at how its constraints can be used to tease and provoke an audience (which, in that opening scene from *Vivre sa Vie*, undoubtedly yearns for a reverse shot that is never granted).

Later in the film, when someone is shot in the street outside the café in which Nana is sitting, Godard chains his camera to Karina, so that we see no more than she does as she rushes to the window (Godard actually stutters the pan from her table to the door, as if to incorporate her stumbling rush in the camera movement). Techniques of this kind can seem merely capricious – the wilful excitement of desire for the sole purpose of denying it – but they also satisfy something else in us, a contentment that the world depicted on the screen conspicuously exceeds the screen itself. At such moments – and in all moments when our perceptions are directed at something we cannot physically see in front of us – cinema unsights in the most fruitful way of all, obscuring for a time the sharp edges where image gives way to darkness.

FREEZE FRAME

There's an intriguing passage in Jean Renoir's autobiography in which he describes how he bartered his cultural patrimony for the raw materials of a new art:

> Since my private means consisted essentially of the pictures bequeathed to me by my father, my excursions into cinema were marked by the disappearance of canvases which were like a part of myself. It was as though a conversation between my father and me had been for ever discontinued. I was living a new version of Balzac's *Peau de Chagrin* and I spent the days brooding over my shame. Every sale seemed to me a betrayal. At night I wandered about my house at Marlotte, of which the walls were being slowly but inexorably stripped bare. I had kept the frames. They were like gaping outlets to a hostile world.

As Renoir's literary allusion acknowledges, there is a pleasingly fabulous symmetry to this tale. In Balzac's novel the magic wild ass's skin of the title shrinks with every wish made upon it; Renoir's artistic desires similarly diminish his artistic inheritance. And for us the story has no real sense of loss because the 'hostile world' didn't have to make the same sacrifice as the son. We gained the films without losing the paintings.

But what's also cherishable about this story is the purity of its oppositions: established masterpieces of fixity and permanence provide the funds for an art of movement and transformation that was still disreputable; a treasure dependent on the value of a unique original pays for the creation of artworks that are themselves dependent for their value on replication. And the artist has to agonize over the soundness of his bargain, an agony that was all the greater because Renoir's early career was not conspicuously successful. The films that the paintings pay for are not those that will make his reputation. August Renoir died

in 1919, some time after his son's infatuation with cinema had
begun but five years before his first active involvement in film-
making, so we can't know how he would have felt about this
filial exchange. But he might not have entirely disapproved.
'Renoir did not insist on absolute immobility,' his son writes
elsewhere, when he is describing sitting for his father. 'Indeed,
I still have a feeling that he feared it.' This provokes another
speculation: why should an artist dedicated to the demanding
task of fixing shimmering life on canvas fear the very condition
of his art? But it also prompts us to ask the question about
cinema itself: does it, too, fear immobility? Once it had
exhausted the sense of overcoming an impotence, did it begin
to dawn that it had also lost a potency – the inherent permanence of the fixed image?

Given cinema's own technological patrimony, its own dependence on an inherited treasure, we can easily bring this question
into slightly sharper focus. Does cinema fear photographs?
According to the proverbial wisdom, the question should hardly
arise. Godard's famous pronouncement that 'Photography is
truth and film is truth twenty-four times a second' proposes a
quite explicit pedigree for cinema's inherited wealth. The phrase
has an economy that was bound to recommend it as tribal
slogan for the Nouvelle Vague, but he wasn't saying anything
particularly new or revolutionary. In his essay on 'The Ontology
of the Photographic Image', André Bazin wrote of photography
as a redeeming invention – one that had freed

> the plastic arts from their obsession with likeness. Painting
> was forced, as it turned out, to offer us illusion and this
> illusion was reckoned sufficient unto art. Photography and
> the cinema, on the other hand, are discoveries that satisfy,
> once and for all and in its very essence, our obsession with
> realism.

For Bazin, as for many others, it is the notional impartiality of
the photograph that represents its supreme virtue. 'For the first
time,' he continues, 'between the originating object and its

reproduction there intervenes only the instrumentality of a non-living agent.' To which one can only reply, echoing the American gun lobby, 'Cameras don't take pictures of people. People do.' But that contradiction would be anachronistic – or at least wouldn't take into account how easy it was in the first decades of photography for the novelty of the mechanism to obscure the ineradicable presence of its operator. So the photograph as unmediated representation of the truth, not to be diluted by montage or camera movement, became the bedrock of Bazin's morality of film.*

And if these statements about truth and reality were simply true themselves you might expect that photographs, as objects within the world depicted by cinema, would enjoy a certain respect onscreen – the deference due to a venerable progenitor. There are, naturally, many cases in which this is exactly how photographs are presented to us in films: as an impeccable record of fact. The cliché of the surveillance photograph in thrillers remains popular to this day, a conspicuously 'artless' sequence of shots (often accompanied by the sound of an automatic shutter-drive as if to underline its dispassionately mechanical selection of moments). Such sequences borrow an idiom from a world of proof, rather than of manufactured reality, and the success of the gesture depends on our acceptance that these shots tell a larger kind of truth, that their deficiency as cinematic images is the very guarantee of their bona fides. The fact that they are often black and white, grainy, ill-framed or with their subject masked by intervening objects only confirms their authority as *found evidence* rather than an artistic arrangement of the world.† Sometimes such photographs will

*What Bazin saw as a liberation, incidentally, Godard recognized might equally be an entrapment: 'We novelists and film-makers are condemned to an analysis of the world, the real; painters and musicians aren't.'
†There is often a curious echo set up between the unawareness of the camera of the actors within such photographs and the unawareness of the camera on which the film's own illusion of overlooked reality depends. The actors who lean over such photographs are themselves subject to surveillance from an offscreen camera, but one that we conspire together to exclude from consciousness.

be introduced as objects within the film – hurled in a casual fan across a policeman's desk, perhaps, or projected on to the screen of a darkened briefing room. On other occasions the spirit of distanced and 'uncontrolling' surveillance will briefly possess the movie camera itself, so that it speaks, like a medium, with a distorted voice. Fluid motion becomes stuttery and fragmented, and the craftsmanship of the image gives way to a functional acceptability.

Such photographs have a paradoxical quality of being both more potent within the texture of the film and less powerful. The affective detachment of photography permits films to include sights that would be intolerable in motion – either outside the commercial limits of decency or a breach of the film's implied contract that it will only show us so much. There is a fine example of this in the 1987 thriller *Best Seller*, a flawed but interesting film in which James Woods attempts to persuade Brian Dennehy's cop turned crime-writer that he is a contract killer. At one point in the film, Woods briefly returns to a contact the two men have left slumped in a photo booth after a beating. You see him feeding quarters into the machine, then the flashes that mark the taking of photographs and finally his emergence to join Dennehy again. When Dennehy asks him what he was doing Woods brushes the question off; but the audience is let in on the secret by means of the strip of photographs that eventually drops into the machine's retrieval slot: a four-shot sequence of the man having his throat cut. The photographs have an evidentiary impact (part of the effectiveness of this implausible scene derives from our sense that they will form a gruesomely unique element in the official dossier of this crime), but they also hold the act at a sufficient distance to make our own vision of it bearable. We aren't obliged to watch something happening before *our* eyes, only something that has already happened in front of the unfeeling eye of an automatic camera. At the same time, the vertical format of those four small frames clearly echoes the stacked images of the strip of film that shows them to us. It effectively invites us to animate a mental movie from these grisly stills.*

In that sequence the photograph tells us the truth in a way that doesn't directly implicate us in the crime, and it fills out a blind spot in the film camera's account of the scene. But there is no shortage of contrary examples either – occasions on which the photograph is introduced in a film as an avatar of falsehood, a deceit that only the motion camera's serial exposures can unveil. Let me offer three particularly notable instances, taken in the order of their making.

The first occurs in Welles's *Touch of Evil*. Janet Leigh has been duped into accompanying a group of Mexican youths who say they have a message from her husband. In fact, this is part of a plot to discredit her. As they reach the door of a tacky hotel, one of the youths puts his arm round her shoulders in an intimate gesture and turns her quickly towards the street. There is a flash as a photograph is taken, and when we see the resulting print its implication is clear: it looks like a picture of a woman with her lover. We know that it is not, but this is why photographs always have the power to betray us, because they isolate

---

*In Brian de Palma's *Blow Out*, this process is actually performed for us in the engrossing sequence in which John Travolta's sound man pieces together a sequence of still photographs of a car crashing into a river to produce a silent movie, to which he then adds the final revelatory touch, a wild track recording that lines up perfectly with this primitive, flick-book movie and exposes the 'accident' as no such thing. In this case the original photographs aren't actively misleading – just insufficient without cinema's power to track trajectories and momentum. A similar antithesis between newsprint photography and film is underlined in Roger Spottiswoode's *Under Fire*. Early in the film Nick Nolte's war photographer is forced to fake a portrait of the dead guerrilla leader, in order to contradict government claims that he has been killed. The dead body is posed with a newspaper and the film freezes briefly as the shutter clicks. Nothing in the 'photograph' we then see contradicts the lie it tells, only the moving frames on either side of that deception. At the end of the film, Nolte's rapid-fire sequence of photographs of a colleague being killed by the security forces is shown as a kind of stop-motion animation. None of the individual frames would supply categorical evidence of what had happened, but arranged in their correct sequence the exact nature of the event becomes clear. These are photographs striving to become film, striving to attain its powers as a reliable witness.

an event from cause and effect. Looking at this image, we see how it would look later and in another place – forcibly separated from its exonerating circumstances.

The second example occurs in a film released just one year after *Touch of Evil*, though many years distant from it in terms of tone and style. Alfred Hitchcock's *North by Northwest* is, among other things, a compendium of misleading appearances: the house to which Cary Grant is taken appears too respectable to be the site of a kidnapping; Grant himself appears to be a paranoid lush rather than the victim of an abduction; the killers' plane at first appears to be crop-spraying; Eva Marie Saint appears to shoot Grant in the Mount Rushmore restaurant. The initiating mistake from which all of these follow occurs when Cary Grant calls out to a passing telegram-boy who has been paging George Kaplan. The coincidence persuades the watching agents that he is the spy they are searching for and Grant's first successful attempt at escape is then thwarted by a far graver case of incriminating appearance, this time given photographic corroboration by Hitchcock. As Grant is telling his story in the United Nations the man he is talking to is stabbed. He bends to help him, withdraws the knife and at that moment is snapped by a passing photographer, alerted by the general shrieks of alarm. We see the resulting picture on the front page of a newspaper reporting the murder: a black-and-white image of Grant wielding the knife, his appeal for a fair hearing converted into a manic stare of aggression. The photograph records what the bystanders in the scene see, and it also preserves the precise moment at which a false impression is made – a false impression that is no longer a matter of furtive misunderstanding but public misapprehension. The photograph allows an untruth to be replicated many times over.*

*Hitchcock is also the source of one of the best cinematic jokes about freeze frame – the gripping climactic scene in *Rear Window*, in which the helpless Jimmy Stewart tries to fend off his murderous neighbour with the only weapon at his disposal, the flash unit on his camera. With each press on the shutter, Raymond Burr stops, momentarily dazzled, but on this occasion Stewart cannot turn life into a photograph, cannot evade the remorseless continuity of the film

144

The final example resists the conventional trope of photography on film – that brief stalling of motion that isolates a durable object from the stream of fugitive impressions that precede and succeed it – but it is equally explicit about its potential mendacity. In Mike Leigh's *Secrets and Lies*, Timothy Spall plays a high street photographer. In one fine montage sequence he is shown at work, coaxing formal simulations of happiness out of customers who bicker and snap and mope. Only a flash marks the moment that will eventually be printed up as a public affidavit of domestic bliss, a decision that emphasizes, in a way that freeze frame would not, the extreme brevity of the smiles Spall traps in his apparatus. It's not particularly surprising, incidentally, to find that some of the very earliest freeze frames in cinema arise from the same circumstances – Robert Siodmak's 1927 film *Menschen am Sonntag* includes a sequence in which Sunday strollers are having their photographs taken and the film freezes to represent the photograph that results. Most directors feel the need for some kind of alibi before they suspend the motion of the picture, and photography offers the most obvious candidate.

These three photographs clearly aren't untrue at one level. In each case they represent an undeniable physical reality: Susan does stand with a stranger's arm draped around her; Roger Thornhill is holding a knife above a fresh corpse (and is, in a much wider sense, responsible for the man's death); the husband did smile briefly at the wife he had just been nagging. But in each case a reliance on the resulting documents would be foolish; they tell lies by a careful exclusion of the context that might help you judge the final image. And in all three cases the cinema-goer is placed in a privileged position with regard to the imagined viewer of the photograph. Still photography is always prone to such falsifications, of course, however pure the

---

that brings Burr ever closer. The sequence recapitulates what we have already been told by the photograph at the very beginning of the film, which shows the wheel from a racing car flying towards the photographer's lens: photography appears to halt the world, but is actually powerless to hold its damage at bay.

original ambitions of its maker, and on rare occasions it is possible to catch it in the act. One of Henri Cartier-Bresson's most famous pictures, of a concentration camp victim denouncing a guard, appears to capture everything about such confrontations in a single image: the rage of the prisoner, the accusing finger, the sneering defiance of the guard. But newsreel footage of the same event, from an almost identical angle, shows that Cartier-Bresson's 'decisive moment' is quite unrepresentative of the encounter, that the guard's 'sneer' is actually an involuntary flinch and that the dramatic gesture of identification is in fact a blow halfway through its trajectory. The picture adds nothing to the scene but stillness and yet it is nevertheless an adulterated account of what actually occurred. Whether Cartier-Bresson captured a larger truth about the opening up of the camps is debatable, but a jurist could not rely on this picture for an account of who did what to whom.*

So a different question might arise about Godard's celebrated statement. His grammar seems to invite an act of mental arithmetic, the sort of virtuous multiplication familiar from advertisements ('Now four times stronger!'). But is the implication really that film has twenty-four times as much truth as photography for any given second? Or is it rather that truth is so perpetually open to revision that only a repeated assay of its constituents will allow us any dependable understanding? Godard's proselytizing text doesn't explicitly refer to the most conspicuous distinction between photography, the begetting medium, and cinema, its triumphant successor. He doesn't, for example, say, 'Photography is truth and film is truth that moves' (even though the emotional pun would have been equally available to him in French). But motion remains the essential burden of his remark, and it is in the combination of photography and

---

*It might seem perverse not to include here a discussion of *Blow-Up*, in which the veracity of a single photograph is entirely central to the film. But the fact that Antonioni's ambiguity is a matter of what can be found hidden in the depths of an image, rather than how it will be interpreted by an objective observer, makes it rather less interesting here than the films I have mentioned.

motion that cinema achieves its catalysing transformation (not the illusion of motion alone, which had been achievable by other devices, and not the photograph's transcription of reality, which had already been commonplace for some time). There is even a hint that early promoters knew how to exploit the vertiginous lurch from a familiar medium to an unfamiliar one that cinema could be made to offer. Writing about his first visit to a cinema, Maxim Gorky describes what seems to be a clever trick of showmanship:

> When the lights go out in the room in which Lumière's invention is shown, there suddenly appears on the screen a large grey picture, 'A Street in Paris' – shadows of a bad engraving. As you gaze at it, you see carriages, buildings and people in various poses, all frozen into immobility. All this is in grey, and the sky above is also grey – you anticipate nothing new in this all too familiar scene, for you have seen pictures of Paris streets more than once. But suddenly a strange flicker passes through the screen and the picture stirs to life. Carriages coming from somewhere in the perspective of the picture are moving straight at you, into the darkness in which you sit.

We can't know whether this teasing moment of disillusion – the audience lulled into thinking that there was nothing new to see here – was planned or inadvertent. Perhaps the projectionist simply hesitated briefly before turning the crank. But it can stand anyway as the first freeze frame, the pioneer of many similar opening sequences in which a photograph thaws into film.* What you have dismissed as a two-dimensional image, fixed and impenetrable, is magically revealed to be a space with depth, into which the camera can travel (or, as Gorky notes, out of which objects may emerge). It isn't simply the lurch out of fixity that gives such moments their dependable jolt of

---

*For my purposes here a freeze frame is any still image that is continuous with a passage of motion, whether it occurs before or after. Stills, which are also relevant to this discussion, are very different in their impact.

pleasure. The transition also draws some of its power from the way in which it transforms the implicit past tense of a photograph into the implied present of the moving image, an effect that is very often emphasized by a fade from black and white or sepia into colour. And these small triumphs over the melancholy that attends all photographs work just as well for a sophisticated audience as they did for the cinematic innocents of the pioneering days.*

But while it isn't difficult to understand why films should use still images as a point of departure, it is a little less obvious why any film, or any director, would willingly relinquish such a cardinal advantage once the film is under way. The 'coming to life' of a still picture is such a dependable way of underlining the vitality of film – its alluring dynamism – that you would think the alternative might be feared as a kind of death. What incentives does it take for cinema to abandon, however briefly, the very ground of its existence, which is the transience of each individual image? It isn't surprising, perhaps, that freeze frames should generally be pressed to the outer edges of films, to those points – at the beginning and the end – that mediate between our ordinary perceptions and the agile transports of the screen, because they so effectively disrupt the illusion of vivacity that has been created. If the unfreezing of a fixed image at the beginning of films registers the lifting of a spell, or the removal

---

*The effect is not always that of time travel, incidentally. Robert Rossen's *The Hustler* includes a credit sequence in which a number of scenes from the film that follows end on a freeze frame. The frames selected are not heroic or pertinent – they seem to stand as a kind of journalistic portfolio and the film implicitly promises to replace such static impressionism with a unified explanation of their meaning. The technique has now degenerated into a cliché of introduction – most commonly seen in television soaps or popular drama, in which the leading characters are often depicted in little vignettes of activity before freezing to create a dramatic portrait. The popularity of this trope may also have something to do with an allusion to the codes of fashion photography, a realm in which the flattering moment, rather than the decisive one, is already a well-established concept. The device was used to just this end in John Schlesinger's *Darling*, a film that purports to be disenchanted with glamour, but cannot ever quite overcome the allure of its leading character.

of the paralysis of history, then what is suggested by freezing it again?

You could frame this question in a different way. We now have some idea of what it is that cinema suspects about photography. It is unsettled by its readiness to treat fragments as if they were wholes and by its inability to take cause and effect into consideration. But the assertion of those disabilities – the rather taunting assertion – only arises, I think, because of the uneasy suspicion that film might also have lost something when it learnt how to move. In short, there must be qualities in the photographic image that the cinema equally *envies* but does not possess. We can explore what they might be by looking more closely at two classic instances in which directors have willingly relinquished the impetus of cinema. Both occur at the end of films and both fully exploit the freeze frame's natural talent for pathos. The first is in François Truffaut's *Les Quatre Cent Coups*, a film that is sometimes wrongly credited as being the first mainstream use of a freeze frame. In 1933 William Dieterle had concluded *Grand Slam*, a light comedy about bridge players, with a sequence that used both slow motion and freeze frame. The process had also been available for years as a way of extending the beat of a sequence, though such uses were not intended to be a conspicuous part of the film's emotional content – or even detectable for that matter. Whatever the claims for precedent, Truffaut's final shot is memorably arresting – an adjective that conventionally implies a rapt immobility in the audience, but that here is just as applicable to the image that fixes us in our seats. Jean-Pierre Léaud, seen running on a beach in a dizzy whirl of liberty, turns to face the camera and is stopped in his tracks. The moment is so canonical, and the film so influential, that it is difficult to think that it might have ended otherwise. But Truffaut's original shooting script reveals that it was not initially conceived of as the film's final frame:

The last image here, Antoine at the shore, becomes a still and fades slowly into another live action shot: Antoine and René walking in the streets of Paris [a shot of them playing hookey, which we have already seen]. As we hear the last words of the commentary, this image also becomes a still, reminding us that it has been taken by a street photographer.

What the commentary was going to say was: 'We are free and far from the tortures of adolescence, but when we walk along the streets we cannot help seeing as accomplices our successors in the third grade, as they begin their 400 blows.'

In the finished version Truffaut abandons the narrative alibi for the still – there can be no street photographers on the beach to account for this sudden stoppage in continuity. He also abandons that trite vocal reassurance – a passage of rueful solidarity that seems to reduce these singular miseries to a generalized and unavoidable rite of passage. The effect in the film as we have it is quite different, a moment that remains poised between Antoine's temporary jubilation and our knowledge that his joyful flight is bound to end. The preservation of his fugitive gesture has the poignancy shared by all photographs: their paradoxical reminder that human flesh does not endure. But this will only go some way to explain the aesthetic thrill an audience is likely to feel at such a moment. Part of this must be physiological. Our brains are adept at projecting motion forwards in time, and so it wouldn't be particularly surprising to find that our minds have anticipated the frames visible on-screen and will already have plotted the likely trajectories of light and shade. And then the body suddenly stops, without deceleration or recoil, freed from the physics that we know all bodies to be subject to.*

There is, of course, a far graver momentum to which we are all subject – that of mortality – and such moments may derive

---

*That edits don't always jar in the same way, even though they involve a similar disruption of anticipated continuity, is because many edits are made with an eye to preserving the movement of a scene across the cut. When an editor or director wishes a cut to make its presence felt they will take care to break such rules of continuity.

some of their sentimental force from the essentially futile attempt to escape from time itself. 'Cinema is the only art which, as Cocteau says . . . "films death at work". Whoever one films is growing older and will die. So one is filming a moment of death at work.' The remark is Godard's* and the implied logic suggests that to freeze the cinematic image should be to suspend the inexorable progress towards death. But the evasion will not work, because photographs achieve their illusion of immortality only at the cost of losing the most basic vital sign of all – movement. As Susan Sontag writes in another context, 'All photographs are *memento mori* . . . Precisely by slicing out this moment and freezing it, all photographs testify to time's relentless melt.' And indeed, although one contemporary described Truffaut's conclusion as a rediscovery of 'real time, that of Mozartian jubilation', it is hard not to feel that the exaltation is poignantly futile. In freeze frame what goes up can stay there, wrenched from a world of consequences. In life it must come down again. Freeze frames briefly oppose the essential evanescence of all cinema images, but they can only do it with a means already understood as grief-prone itself. They remind you that while film is almost never a *nature morte* (as the French call a still life), the best it can offer is nature in the process of dying.†

This evasion is much more explicit in the second freeze frame I want to consider, which concludes George Roy Hill's affectionately revisionist Western *Butch Cassidy and the Sundance Kid*. Like Truffaut's final shot, this image has achieved a certain

---

Godard on Godard: Critical writings by Jean-Luc Godard, Da Capo Press, 1986.

†In an intriguing essay on this subject in *Persistence of Vision*, Garrett Stewart argues that photographs are almost *always* a correlative of death when they are used in film. He cites persuasive cases from Max Ophuls's *Letter from an Unknown Woman* and Terrence Malick's *Badlands*, among other films, but his concentration on death narrows the affective force of photographs too much. It's true that our inexorable advancement towards death is what gives memories their poignancy, but an account of photographs in films that doesn't also consider cinema's anxiety about its own permanence as an art form has left out something important. This is an issue of 'truth to life' as well as 'truth to death'.

fame. Unlike Truffaut's, it employs a specifically photographic idiom – that of a sepia wash – to explain its interruption of fluency. Holed up in a Bolivian town, surrounded by hundreds of troops, Butch and Sundance are clearly doomed. They are already wounded and while they pay a wry lip-service to the notion of escape, discussing the strategy of their break-out, it is clear that this final act is a kind of defiant suicide, a fatal repetition of the dangerous synchronized leap they make earlier in the film when cornered by a posse on a cliff-top. Hill cuts from a shot taken inside the building of the two men plunging into the dazzling vacancy of a sunlit door to what at first appears to be a medium reverse angle of them emerging. Then as the sound of massed gunfire continues the image freezes and fades to sepia. With a piano playing an elegiac tune, the camera pulls back, leaving the two figures centred in the square. The director has erected a monument to his characters, one that coincidentally spares us from confronting the undignified reality of their death – blood and brain matter and a swarm of flies. As a way of 'biting the dust', this offers the great virtue of not getting any unsightly grit on that expensive and bankable dentistry.

This isn't the first use of sepia tone in the film, nor the first employment of an image that does not move. When the outlaws decide to leave the West for Bolivia, their passage by way of nineteenth-century New York is represented by a montage of period photographs – many of them real ones into which the actors have been carefully insinuated, so that Paul Newman, Katherine Ross and Robert Redford can be seen peering from a rowing boat in nineteenth-century Central Park, or surrounded by long-dead revellers at Coney Island. These offer a series of formal poses, faces turned towards the camera, aware of the need to hold still for its deficient vision, but they are also a register of the film's documentary pretensions.

Butch Cassidy and the Sundance Kid is a mild-mannered example of the widespread disavowal of mythic Western archetypes that was so fashionable at the end of the sixties, but it is not one that wishes to risk any sourness. It will introduce a bicycle to its setting (for a particularly saccharine musical interlude), and it will remind you of how close a stiff-collared urban civilization was to the mythically atemporal space of the Western, but it will not yield up its heroes. The last shot fixes them in perpetuity (or at least the cinema's best approximation to it). Their guns are smoking and their eyes are narrowed against the glare.

Someone naturally had to choose which frame to freeze, whether it was Hill himself or his editor Richard C. Meyer, and it's only fair to say – whatever one's reservations about the film that precedes it – that it was chosen well. Redford has just fired the gun in his right hand so that a plume of blue smoke still hangs over both men's heads; Newman has just raised his right hand to fire again, drawing a strong line to the upper left-hand corner of the screen. Their eye lines are directed outwards, and their bodies incline in mirrored sympathy, slightly to the right and left. Both men are on one foot, in positions that are off-balance, but in compositional terms they create a perfect equilibrium, an epitome of stoical grace.* As a piece of sentimental statuary it is mendacious but effective – even when detached from the affections the film might have aroused in a viewer.

The word 'epitome' has the Greek word for cutting at its root (it literally means an abridgement), and in such images – a single frame excised from the many that make up the heroes' last run – you have a vivid reminder of the way in which an essence must cut away extraneous details. And that moment of physical grace, an unpredictable gesture isolated by the freeze frame, is even more poignant because we know that nothing that follows is likely to obey the expected rules of momentum.

---

*The true freeze frame is never a pose, even if the end result might display composure. In the best freeze frames – and despite their strong element of contingency it is possible to discriminate – there should always be a sense that the image is on its way to being something else but that this interim moment offers its own revelation. It is a negotiation between the entirely accidental and the carefully calculated.

We cannot be sure when the first bullets will strike or how they will make the bodies jerk and spin.

Most viewers will not need to elaborate their responses to this photograph from scratch (it clearly is a photograph by now, announced by the posthumous sepia that has replaced living colour, and that creates an entirely anachronistic artefact within the film – a nineteenth-century, fast-shutter-speed action shot). In fact, they will have had several opportunities to rehearse their feelings about men captured in the immanence of death, and those opportunities will have been provided almost entirely from documentary photography. Hill does not take Robert Capa's much debated photograph of a Spanish Republican falling in battle as his model, though a less commercially nervous film might easily have done so, leaving us with Butch and the Kid in the gracelessness of death, limbs flailing in response to quite exterior impulses. (Capa's famous picture is clearly an influence on just such a freeze frame at the end of Peter Weir's *Gallipoli*.) It's possible, though, that someone had a real image in mind, because there are photographic doppelgängers for the dynamic tilt of this last frame, including one of Don McCullin's pictures of street fighting in Limassol in 1964, which offers a strikingly similar combination of urgent slant, white plaster wall, dark doorway and gun. This is almost certainly a coincidence of artistic selection rather than a confirmed paternity. Both Hill and McCullin are responding to similar instincts about the composition of a dramatic image, and both are required to choose from a sequence. But the similarity takes us back to the question with which we began: what is it about still photography that film envies?

At least part of the answer must lie, I think, in the ability of a photograph to remain composed beneath an admiring gaze. Where the still photograph has a durable presence as an artistic object, the cinema image is always on the run, always giving way to a successor, always pressed for time. Indeed, it's one of the paradoxes of cinema that its clarity of sight arises out of a sequence of pictures *none of which is seen clearly*. The physiology of forward and backward masking – by which two rapidly sequential images interfere with the perception of one or other – ensures that any single frame is always mediated by those before and after it. Susan Sontag betrays an interesting prejudice in this regard when she writes, in *On Photography*, of television as 'a stream of underselected images, each of which cancels its predecessor'. Exactly the same can be said of film, though film is rather less susceptible to cultural bullying than television. And when a film freezes (or unfreezes, in the case of the openings we've already discussed), at least some of the ready pathos of the device derives not from the particular subject matter involved – people elated and doomed to disappointment or people vividly alive and doomed to die – but from the sudden confrontation of two entirely disparate forms of photographic record. Narrative film exists in a virtual present tense. Even when we watch Buster Keaton in *The General* we do not have the sense of watching a record of something that happened either fifty years ago, when the film was made, or even 135 years ago, during the American Civil War of the film's setting. We accept at some level that the tale is unwinding right now. We accept that, for a time at least, Keaton lives again. If this weren't true, tension and expectation would be all but impossible in the cinema. Photographs, by contrast, are always an opening into the past – what appears in them consigned irretrievably to history. (This is true even of instant photographs, which have the odd capacity to make you wistful about what is right in front of your eyes, tugged by the awareness that the original has already begun to depart from the recording, opening a gap that can only grow larger as time passes.) So the abrupt conjunction of the two involves us in an instantaneous passage from one time-scale to another. It is as if the freeze frame offers us the ability to feel nostalgia for the present.

The endings of both *Les Quatre Cents Coups* and *Butch Cassidy and the Sundance Kid* raise another matter, too: the differing notions of the photogenic that photography and film throw up. Every freeze frame poses an academic question for

the audience and a professional one for the editor or director:
why this frame, in particular, and not the one that comes next,
or in another second and a half? Because the truth is that what
is worth filming and what is worth photographing are only
likely to coincide at very special moments. A film sequence is
representationally 'robust', in the sense that it can survive
moments of awkwardness or inadvertence, because it passes so
rapidly through them. You might think of it as a car driving at
speed along a corniche road and plunging in and out of tunnels
– the sunshine and the view are likely to prevail over the concrete as long as the speed is right and the tunnels not too long.
The photograph, on the other hand, is 'brittle'; however short
the tunnels are, if the shutter is triggered at the wrong moment
then the result is not just slightly deficient, it is useless. You
could put this another way by saying that we expect more of a
photographic image than we do of any single frame of a movie,
which is no problem in normal circumstances, when no single
frame will stay still long enough for us to bring such critical
attention to bear. Films skate on thin ice, in this respect, and if
they stop they must ensure that they do so on something that
will bear the unsupported weight of the audience's attention.
When they specifically choose not to – as in the case of *The
Hustler*, where the still images offer no conspicuous content but
their own arbitrariness – then the film will be making some
kind of case for its ability to fill out that fragmentary vision.
But for the most part, the freeze frame inevitably proposes that
this moment is distinguished – that it aspires to permanence
and must pass a more rigorous inspection. This particular pause
is always pregnant.

There are directors, of course, who decline to implicate the
machinery of cinema in their creation of significant stillness –
Ozu Yasujiro and Robert Bresson come to mind as examples of
directors who are at pains to deny the audience's expectations
that moving pictures will always move. But such asceticism will
always risk looking like a mistrust of the medium rather than
a pleasure in its possibilities. Writing about Bresson in his essay

on transcendental style in the cinema,* Paul Schrader notes that 'by denying a motion picture its motion, he spurns the most basic of cinematic screens' (a remark in which 'screens' is used to refer to the conventions that intervene between a viewer and the emotional content of the film). The mischievously ingenuous might point out that without a screen you don't see a thing but, in truth, Bresson doesn't dispose of it at all. If we are to notice that it is missing we principally need to be aware of its existence, and those passages where movement is in suspension – rather than artificially arrested by a freeze frame – work only because human will is so conspicuously at work.

It may be helpful here to consult a pre-photographic thinker about such matters – one undazzled by the peculiar epistemological charms of photography. In his essay 'Laocoön', Gotthold Lessing also engages in an act of comparative criticism. His work is sub-titled 'The limits of painting and poetry', and it reflects on the differing opportunities open to the visual and the literary artist. The question of representation is the crucial one, in particular the representation of violent action, which is exemplified, in his case, by the famous statue of Laocoön and his sons being attacked by a sea serpent.

> If the artist can never, in presence of ever-changing Nature, choose and use more than one single moment, and the painter in particular can use this single moment only from one point of vision; if, again, their works are made not merely to be seen, but to be considered, to be long and repeatedly contemplated, then it is certain that that single moment can never be chosen too significantly.

This anxiety might be thought to be irrelevant to film, where moments isolated in their singularity are rare and will anyway be whisked away from you at the film-maker's pleasure, but Lessing still has things to tell a cinematic reader (he was, as it

*Transcendental Style in Film: Ozu, Bresson, Dreyer, Paul Schrader, Da Capo Press, 1988.

157

happens, one of those pre-film writers that Eisenstein admitted
as a kind of virtuous heathen of cinematography, along with
Dickens and Leonardo da Vinci).

Lessing addresses the problem of selection like this:

Now that alone is significant and fruitful which gives free
play to the imagination. The more we see, the more must we
be able to add by thinking. The more we add thereto by
thinking, so much the more can we believe ourselves to see.
In the whole gamut of an emotion, however, there is no
moment less advantageous than its topmost note. Beyond it
there is nothing further, and to show us the uttermost is to
tie the wings of fancy and oblige her, as she cannot rise above
the sensuous impression, to busy herself with weaker pictures
below it, the visible fullness of expression acting as a frontier
which she dare not transgress. When, therefore, Laocoön
sighs, the imagination can hear him shriek; but if he shrieks,
then she cannot mount a step higher from this representation,
nor again, descend a step lower without seeing him in a more
tolerable and consequently more uninteresting condition. She
hears him only groan, or she sees him already dead.

It should be immediately clear that cinema has a very different
relation to these aesthetic strictures than any other form of
visual depiction. Lessing's dicta may hold good for some forms
of still photography, but are made redundant by cinema, which
can show the struggle of Laocoön in all its sequential variety –
cutting close as the jaws clamp on flesh, pulling back to reveal
the roiling contortions of competing muscles. It still must keep
a wary eye on unintentional comedy, but the anxieties of
depicting such a scene are bound to rest more on the 'realistic'
motion of the sequence than the implications of any single
gesture. Indeed, Lessing beautifully describes the advantages of
cinema in this respect (though he has a poet in mind rather
than a director).

Nothing requires the poet to concentrate his picture on one

single moment. He takes up each of his actions, as he likes, from its very origin and conducts it through all possible modifications to its final close. Every one of those modifications, which would cost the artist an entire separate canvas or marble block, cost the poet a single line; and if this line, taken in itself, would have misled the hearer's imagination, it was either so prepared for by what preceded, or so modified and supplemented by what followed, that it loses its separate impression, and in its proper connection produces the most admirable effect in the world.

Just as *North by Northwest* sets 'proper connections' against the misled imagination of those who take the newspaper photograph as proof of Cary Grant's guilt, so the poet can continuously modify the effects of his single line.

This does raise for some observers an anxiety about the nature of the film audience's contemplation. How is it possible for the viewer to meditate on an image that will not remain still for a second, indeed that only rests onscreen for less than a forty-eighth of a second? (The twenty-four frames that occupy a second of film are each shown twice and every one is also separated by a moment of darkness.) And if contemplation of that kind is not possible, then what precisely is our imagination acting upon?

Roland Barthes approaches the problem in his essay 'The Third Meaning', in which he meditates himself on a number of stills from Eisenstein's *Ivan the Terrible* and *The Battleship Potemkin*. Barthes's argument is an abstruse one – particularly because a certain amount of irresolvable enigma is one of the components of the 'third meaning' he proposes – but it's easy to read it as a losing attempt to grapple both with the troubling surfeit of any photography and the fugitive nature of the cinema image. The resulting piece is a little like the statue of Laocoön itself: the critic entangled in the coils of a monstrous paradox.

'Third meanings' (Barthes's clearest example is a contingent symmetry on the face of a grieving old woman in *The Battleship*

Potemkin) offer possibilities of distraction from the intentional codes of the artist – those that are calculatedly aimed at an audience's interpretative instinct. Barthes locates the purely filmic within this third meaning ('the filmic is that in the film which cannot be described, the representation which cannot be represented'), but what's interesting about his essay for our purposes is his concession that this third level of meaning is effectively invisible in moving pictures. 'To a certain extent [the extent of our theoretical fumblings] the filmic, very paradoxically, cannot be grasped in the film "in situation", "in movement", "in its natural state", but only in that major artefact, the still.' Barthes doesn't make it entirely clear what he has in mind by 'still' here – the images he is discussing at the beginning of his essay are clearly single-frame blow-ups from Eisenstein's films – but he later talks of his passion for the kinds of still one sees outside a cinema or in film magazines.

This is to blur a crucial distinction, because 'stills' in the latter sense (the sense of publicity) are quite different in their nature from stills in the first sense. They are taken by a specialist photographer, operating during or just after a take, and they frequently involve a conscious suspension of motion on the part of the actors – a pose, in short. What's more, a collection of stills offers a formal proposal of the film's virtues rather than an illustrative abstraction of them. This is why stills so often have a faintly cataleptic or ceremonial air – a sense of stiffness that has not been imposed by the machinery of the camera shutter, but by the contractual obligations of the performers to 'do it one more time for the stills'. 'The' still in this sense is a quite different object of contemplation to 'a' still (indeed, it would be revealing to compare the two forms in the case of a classic movie – setting the mercantile frieze of poses intended for the foyer of a cinema against the mobile, elusive original projected inside).

Lessing's act of imagination and Barthes's act of speculative criticism both need a kind of stillness to function properly – in Lessing's case because imagination is enfranchised, in a strictly controlled way, by an absence of narrative information; in Barthes's case because he wants time to stray from the route marked out by the film-maker (he was never exactly an obedient tourist and writes almost frantically in another place of film as 'without remission, a continuum of images; the film follows, like a garrulous ribbon). The unyielding itinerary of a film, moving us on to the next sight at the director's disposition, is intolerant of such private excursions. But in both cases the absence of motion doesn't just adjust the audience's responses (slowing them down, say); it radically alters the nature of the response required. And one is tempted – despite the hazards of such generalizations – to venture the following: that the more a film wishes to exploit the fruitful ambiguity of an image (rather than the narrative ambiguity of a plot or the psychological ambiguity of a performance, both of which take place in time) the further it will retreat from motion.*

The film that undoubtedly permits the greatest degree of contemplation on these matters is Chris Marker's *La Jetée*, a half-hour science-fiction film that is composed entirely of stills (there is one brief exception to this rule). On first seeing the film you might be tempted to describe it as an experiment in cinema, such is the perverse focus of its self-denial. In other words, you might mistakenly assume that cinematic motion was the only object of its curiosity and its banishment a kind of test

*Of course, it's still the case that cinema is dependent on still images – literally could not do without them. And this is true not just in the sense that a film requires a very large number of still pictures to create its illusion of motion but because the editing process implies a large number of choices about which frames are going to form the limits to each uncut sequence. On an editing table the film 'freezes' repeatedly, as it must do in order for an incision to be made (an incision that must slice between one frame and the next, except in the case of optical fades). It's true that these notional stills (which will be seen only by the editor in their full immobility) are different from those that occur visibly within a film. They are selected not for their unique virtues as symbolic gesture or epitome, but because of their ability to form a relationship with the frame to which they will be spliced – an arranged marriage that is usually based on some notion of compatibility. What's more, the greater the incompatibility between the two images, the larger is the kinetic effect of their forced union.

– the director merely pulling the wings off flies to see whether they can survive. But *La Jetée* has no particular hypothesis to prove, and its method turns out to be bonded so securely to its subject matter that the two are quite indivisible. The stilled frames from which the story is retrieved cannot be read as a device applied to the tale, in order to rescue it from banality or ordinariness; rather they stir in us frustrations and desires that are very similar to those experienced by the central character. It is, you might say, a film in which the shooting style, rather than any particular camera angle, offers a point-of-view perspective. *La Jetée* tells the story of a temporal paradox: a character haunted by a childhood memory of seeing a man killed, who eventually discovers, after travelling through time, that it is his own death he has witnessed. Marker begins the film with a voiced epigraph: 'Nothing distinguishes memories from ordinary moments. Only afterwards do they claim remembrance, on account of their scars.' An opposition of undifferentiated flux and isolated fragments is immediately established – an opposition for which we can quite easily substitute the perceived fluidity of cinema and the fragmentary nature of photography.

The images Marker employs vary considerably in the nature of their stillness. Some are shots of static, lifeless landscapes (Paris, devastated by an atomic war) in which the stillness is the burden of the picture (that is, if these scenes were to be filmed conventionally they would remain still, though a tiny scrap of paper might flicker in the foreground to offset the terrifying absence of human motion). Then there are shots that occupy an ambiguous middle ground (a piercing look from one of the masked survivors who are conducting experiments in time-travel, for instance, which could be an intimidating stare or a moment seized from a quite unthreatening movement). Finally, there are sequences in which motion is inescapably the central motif (most notably in a shot of pigeons taking to the air, their wings moving so fast that they have evaded the shutter's ability to catch a clear outline).

In addition to demonstrating just how wide a range of dyna-
misms the photograph can offer, Marker also explores the
expressive nature of the edits between his frames. In some cases
the rhythm is processional and regular (like a photo-romance
in which all the boxes are of equal size), but at other times –
most particularly when the time-traveller is coming closer to
his elusive goal of contact with a woman on the other side of
the temporal divide – you are offered more rapid successions
of images. Marker takes the longing of the film spectator to be
released into the immediacy of motion and uses it to evoke the
aching desire of his hero for a genuine sense of contact. But
this is not an opportunistic exploitation of a sensation that just
happens to come easily to hand. We seek a virtual present just as
he does; we want to get beyond the implied past tense of
the photographic image just as he wishes to break through the
apparently impenetrable wall between now and then. The
images begin to blur into each other (a stop-motion with faded
transitions rather than hard cuts), which is tantalizing in its
proximity to natural movement. When the women opens her
eyes in the film's only moving sequence, the motion still appears
faintly retarded, a little stutter of stiffness, but the moment is
very poignant all the same – for those inside and outside the
film's created world it marks the consummation of a desire.

It clearly isn't accidental that Marker's film contains many
isolated images of sculpture. These partly register as an
expression of intangible beauty (you can touch a sculpture but
never – outside of myth – the body it depicts), but they also
reinforce the sense that the film is about the way in which
memory operates anyway, preserving its treasures as frozen
gestures rather than animatronic tableaux that would be
doomed to repeat their looped motions endlessly in the mind.
The voice-over refers speculatively at one point to the 'museum
of memory', introducing a sequence of fixed shots of statues.
Later the time-traveller and the woman he is attempting to get
close to walk round a natural history museum, crammed with
stuffed birds and animals, many of them mounted in a simul-

ation of vivacity; birds have their wings spread as if they are just about to take flight and the echo of scattering pigeons from earlier in the film invites you to make an association between this morbid act of preservation and the still life of the camera. What exactly are we to make of the repeated shots of the woman – slight smile on her lips, hair lifted by the breeze like feathers feeling the air? Are those images statuary or taxidermy, and which would be preferable – the simulation of beauty or an artificial prevention of its decay? The alternative poses a profound question about the nature of our memories, which must always corrupt what is remembered.

La Jetée's allusions to the Pygmalion myth follow the conventional direction of travel: the time-traveller wants to release the woman from the state of petrifaction in which she is trapped by his memory. But photography frequently involves a reversal of that myth. The artist seeks to make a permanent object out of a perishable beauty, and cinema is not immune to the same temptation for all its powers of movement. In her influential essay on 'Visual Pleasure in Narrative Cinema', Laura Mulvey appears to treat this as an exercise in gender power: 'The presence of woman is an indispensable element of spectacle in normal narrative film, yet her visual presence tends to work against the development of a story line, to freeze the flow of action in moments of erotic contemplation.' This is well observed, I think – though we might hesitate about some of the details. The choice of 'woman' (an abstraction) rather than 'women' (particular individuals) makes the statement a touch grander than it really needs to be. But this way of saying that films are prone to pause over the features of their leading ladies reasonably alerts you to the way in which such moments often feature as interruptions of the business at hand.

Sometimes, of course, the business at hand might be what the woman in question is feeling, in which case a close-up can't necessarily be treated as inimical to the flow of narrative. What's more, there are uncomplicated technical reasons why close-ups are susceptible to a certain immobility: the frame is tighter and necessarily holds the object it encloses in a gentle but firm grasp. (DeMille actually banned the use of moving backgrounds in his close-ups because it distracted the eye from the intended object of contemplation.)

But such qualifications don't undermine the central point: that film makes sculptures of the objects it places on display within the cabinet of the screen. They are lit in such a way that their sculptural qualities are emphasized, which may in turn impose a further fixity on the living actress – if you have spent an hour bringing Garbo's face into just the right balance of light and shade, the very last thing you will want is that she should animate those features with a thought or a word. Indeed, when Reuben Mamoulian transformed Garbo into a kind of tragic figurehead at the end of *Queen Christina*, he made it clear that he wanted a void on which the sentiments of the audience could be inscribed, a freeze frame created through sheer muscular will: 'I want your face to be a blank piece of paper,' he said. 'I want the writing to be done by every member of the audience. I'd like it if you could avoid blinking your eyes, so that you're nothing but a beautiful mask.' As that direction reminds us, such sculptures are fragile if presented in motion, and require a considerable amount of muscular discipline to prevent their dissolution. The stillness you see (distinguished from photography by the irrepressible tremors of life) represents a matter of will or surrender on the part of an individual that intensifies the image's sense of transcendence.

The poignancy of the final frames of *Queen Christina* derives not just from the sadness of Garbo's bereavement (her lover has been murdered just as she abdicates to join him in exile) but from the way in which the film fulfils her greatest fear, both as the character and the actress who played her. 'I am tired of being a symbol,' she has complained to her Chancellor earlier, 'I long to be a human being.' The distinction between those two fates is explicitly defined by her as the difference between motion and a kind of perpetual immobility: 'A symbol is eternal, changeless, an abstraction. A human being is mortal and changeable.' At the moment of its greatest sympathy for the Queen's human plight, the film deprives her of precisely those qualities, transforming her from wounded individual to an abstraction of sorrow. And yet it is only through such petrifaction that she achieves a fixed place in our memories – an image that can dependably be summoned when someone says 'Garbo'.

There is a rather more convoluted approach to such matters in Truffaut's *Jules et Jim*, which also alludes to the Pygmalion myth – through the conceit that Catherine represents the living embodiment of a statue the two men have seen on holiday in Greece. In *The World Viewed*, Stanley Cavell describes the sequence of swift freeze frames of Catherine as follows:

> [T]he image private to the two men appears as if materialized by their desire, which freezes her at the height of her laughter, from which she then descends. So the image confirms not only her identity with the figure they first saw in her – the statue they had gone in search of come to life . . . but also the fact that she is their creation, their greatest work as artists.

This is only half right. Truffaut's freeze frames do reduce Catherine briefly to the status of aesthetic object, a beautiful thing to be looked at (and potentially possessed), rather than the evasive and complex person she proves to be. But the fact that these freeze frames occur in the middle of an uncut passage (in other words, the image freezes only briefly before restoring her vitality to her) serves as an assertion of her mobility as much as of the men's sexual captivation – the effect is of a woman repeatedly escaping a gaze that tries to pin her down. Cavell's description implies that the freeze frame is superimposed on her by Truffaut as a thematic signpost, a kind of supervisory instruction about how we are to look at her. But it is equally possible that the sudden daze of cessation (freeze frames always impart a little blow) represents a temporary stupefaction on the men's part – the sense most of us have felt of being briefly abstracted from time by a particular sight.

In *Casino*, a film much bound up with the expressive possibilities of the freeze frame, Scorsese includes an almost identical device when he shows Sam Rothstein's first encounter with Ginger McKenna, the beautiful hustler with whom he falls in love. Ginger's behaviour is flagrant, attracting the attention of everyone in the gaming room, and Scorsese cuts between shots of Rothstein looking on unmoving (his own stillness is that of commanding self-discipline) and her own pirouetting exhibitionism. The moment that Scorsese chooses to freeze is one of the least dynamic in the sequence – not when Ginger's arms are thrown in the air as she hurls chips across the room, but when she subsides to consider what she's achieved. The freeze depicts her in a moment of serenity – a calm centre to the storm around her, which is partly a representation of her character and partly a representation of Sam's vision of her. But his admiration cannot permanently arrest her, only impede her; in the next sequence she moves in slow motion, natural sound faded beneath music to isolate her further from the scrambling turmoil around her. 'What a move,' says Sam on the voice-over, stressing her motion as the essence of her attraction. 'I fell in love right there.' Another tension is aroused in us here also: the unsatisfactory choice we sometimes have to make between looking at beauty and living with it. The freeze frame permits (and sometimes expresses) a gaze that is detached from the necessity for response or reaction. It appears at a moment when, for Sam, Ginger is little more than a pretty picture. But his proper knowledge of what moves her – rather than what it is about her that moves him – can only unwind through time.*

*This might seem a lot for a single frame to achieve, but Scorsese is fully aware of just how adaptable a device freeze frame is. There are at least ten occasions when *Casino* discards the power of movement: at times to hold a fugitive detail for our observation, as when a money-counter furtively pockets a bill or when Sam's tight smile betrays the insincerity of a politic compliment; at other times in the more conventional cinematic trope of the photograph, as when Ginger's meeting with Nicky Santoro is depicted through a telephoto lens which freezes to the sound of a motor-driven shutter. Perhaps its most striking use, though, is a brief scene in which another gangster is asked whether Nicky is having an affair with Sam's wife. He knows that she is, but this is a breach of mob manners that will have grave consequences for Nicky if it emerges; on the other hand, if he lies about it and is found out he will be in danger. Scorsese

The kind of conspicuous technique Scorsese displays here and elsewhere is likely to raise a question of purity with many viewers. There are moments when the stuttering hesitations of Scorsese's camera seem to say no more than 'Don't forget, in your excitement, that all this is made from a ribbon of celluloid.'* Certainly there is a point of view that would regard such devices as improperly cosmetic; the very word 'device' carries an undertow of stratagem or trickery. But there are good grounds for rejecting such a crude distinction between the natural and the contrived. Not the least of them is that our perception of motion is itself a mental reconstruction. In more than one case, localized brain injuries have left their victims with a kind of stroboscopic vision. H.L. Tauber reports a patient for whom a moving motorcycle appears as a set of overlapping images, none of which is in motion, while neuroscientist Colin Blakemore has written of a case in which a brain-damaged woman sees a cup of tea being poured as a set of discrete 'stills', in each of which the level of liquid has risen slightly. Such pathologies suggest that, while seamless motion may be a property of the world, it is not necessarily an inescapable part of our perception of it. It may be that the freeze frame's essentially metaphorical construction of emotional meanings works so well because it touches on a subconscious physiological truth.

In any case, the theoretical distinction between a non-

---

presents the scene in three still images, a frozen two-way which allows the actor to talk you through the literally dreadful hiatus of deliberation – as he decides to lie and thus risk his own life. The freeze frame here is effectively a close-up of a private moment of paralysis, where movement in any direction is just as hazardous. Nor is that the limit of Scorsese's inventions. Elsewhere he even uses a brief flashback freeze frame after a shooting, showing you the foil-wrapped sandwich that a nervous policeman had mistaken for a gun – a kind of microscopic section of flurried vision. Virtually no aspect of the director's ability to manipulate time is left out.

*Scorsese's freeze frames sometimes operate like a survivable equivalent of that fatal halt that many older film-goers will have experienced at some time or other. The sound groans to silence and the fixed image takes on an ominous brightness, then the emulsion begins to bubble and the picture blackens and retreats from the scorching brilliance that is the ground of its existence.

intrusive director and a manipulative one (the adjective is not an insult, to my mind) is likely to break down on close inspection. It's true that there are film-makers who dedicate themselves to a simplicity of photographic representation, but in many cases they have merely relocated the strong-arming of the director to some space outside the frame. The uninflected vision offered by a Bresson film is dependent on an intensity of artistic control (or tyranny, if you prefer) that would make Scorsese look positively laissez-faire. That the authority is asserted before the shutter opens, rather than later, in the editing room, may seem too subtle a distinction to audiences who are, in both cases, obliged to take what they are given. But as a technique, freeze frame is open to suspicion precisely because the word technique can uncontroversially be applied – because it is an effect of cinema that is accessible at the push of a button, in a way that a glancing brilliancy of performance or a compositional insinuation is not. And techniques are generally taken to stand in opposition to inspirations; they are a means that offer no guarantee of the ends to which they are put. Like slow motion – that other assertion of cinema's ability to control time – the freeze frame can seem too promiscuous in its readiness to supply an effect. There are good grounds for a wariness about its use, but the suspicion of what is perceived as merely technological is a curious prejudice in an art so utterly dependent on machinery. (You can put on a play without costumes, lighting or a theatre; you can find a readership for a book with nothing more elaborate for a printing press than a few sheets of carbon paper, but film cannot exist apart from the mechanisms of photography and projection.)

Fear and envy meet in these suspicions – a recognition that cinema surrenders something vital of itself when it surrenders motion and a resentment of the undeniable impact of those moments when it does. 'When a director dies, he becomes a photographer,' said the British documentarist John Grierson, in the course of a disapproving comment on Von Sternberg's meticulously composed aestheticism in *Shanghai Express*. A fate at least as bad as death, this implies, if not actually worse. But even if you share the exasperation with Von Sternberg's preciosity about the projected image, it's possible to rehabilitate the freeze frame – and to convey something of its emotional possibilities – by thinking of a non-technological counterpart.

When Fred Astaire dances, his routines often include moments of suspension or poise, a hesitation in his fluency that you might be tempted to read as a stutter or a block, but for the beauty of the gesture and the fact that it syncopates with such assurance. Why is this moment so intoxicating, when it interrupts the real expression of skill? It is partly because it advertises the headlong daring of the dance, in which every step must lead to the next without a stumble, partly because it briefly reasserts the human management of this apparently effortless flow. These brief arrests are statements about motion, not about immobility, and it is important that they are negotiations with the bodily facts of weight and impetus. They cannot last too long, or they would break the rhythm of what we have really come to see. But they cannot be too short either, or we won't have the pleasure of cessation in the midst of movement. The best freeze frames onscreen achieve something similar: they rest briefly outside cinema, only the better to admire its compelling and effortless motion.

THE SMALL SCREEN

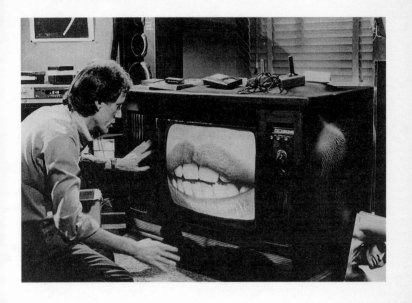

Let us begin with a shudder in Hollywood, an involuntary reflex from an industry dedicated to making others jump. For decades this small area of seismically unreliable real estate had bent itself to the production of every known variety of human agitation – the quiver of desire, the startled flinch, the tremor of helpless laughter. But this time it was Hollywood that found itself prone to odd, spasmodic movements. A new arrival had threatened it and the responses looked distinctly like panic. At first there are sudden and violent changes of shape; Cinemascope, Vistavision, Technirama and other new formats expand the screen so that the actors are either left stranded in a desert of unaccustomed space or obliged by uncertain directors to drape themselves horizontally across the frame. But other symptoms reveal themselves too – all part of a highly strung attempt to reinforce the hitherto uncontested supremacy of cinematic representation. Green and red celluloid glasses are issued to audiences, so that objects onscreen can swing out at the viewers, forcing them to duck their heads. And there is even more embarrassing evidence of fright. Take Aromarama, for example, which was developed by the inventor Charles Weiss to add scent to the two senses already served by film.*

The provocation for all this defensive aggression, from the sudden swelling of screen ratios to the alarmed discharge of smells, was the increasing vigour of television – the first medium to mount an effective rivalry for the eyes of the paying public. However irrational some of these reactions may appear now,

*Though Aroma-rama wasn't a huge success, it was used in 1959 to add verisimilitude to a documentary film about China called *Behind the Great Wall* – whether the olfactory repertoire included the pungent whiff of night-soil isn't recorded. Similarly, William Castle, an ingenious showman director, introduced dubious audiences to 'Percepto' – a system in which an electric buzzer goosed paying selected customers for *The Tingler*, a rare example of a producer taking steps to get bums off seats.

the fear itself was certainly not. From the boom years just after the war, when weekly audiences averaged around 87 million, cinema was to lose patronage steadily; some twenty years later the weekly audience was about a sixth of the size. For the first time the cinema's monopoly on the moving image was threatened and, as evidence grew that the rival was both powerful and durable, cinema reacted in the only ways available to it. The first of those was the almost hysterical flutter of spurious self-improvement described above – a scramble to distance itself from the new arrival in ways that could not be emulated in the home – either through sheer size of the screen or through the sheer scale of the events depicted upon it.

Changing social attitudes were of some assistance to cinema. A 1952 ruling by the Supreme Court confirmed that the Free Speech amendment to the Constitution applied to films as well as the press, a decision that liberated producers to introduce more adult material and opened up another front in the war against television.

As in all wars there were some attempts at collaboration too; for a short time some cinemas were equipped to screen television as a theatrical experience, a quixotic alliance that very quickly fizzled out. And while the major companies ensured that their contracted stars would not appear on the small screen (and initially refused to sell the rights to their film catalogues), almost all of them attempted to invest in their new competitor.

But if cinema could not ultimately win this battle it could take its revenge, something it has done since with a cold and steady determination.* The small screen was to be represented

*Does it make sense to characterize cinema as a single entity here, an organism with its own instincts and emotions? Well, it's clear that such a passage can't stand as anything but a metaphor, but the metaphor may alert us to something important. There are filaments of influence and common feeling that connect one film to another, and if such connections never quite amount to a neural network capable of expressing fears and hopes, they can nonetheless create a detectable shape, a trace of some shared anxiety. Such is the case with Hollywood's treatment of television, in which historical prejudices survive long beyond the time when there is a genuine economic justification for them.

on the large one (and almost invariably still is today) as aesthetically deficient, emotionally parasitic, and socially corrupting. It was in the nature of these charges that they were often self-contradicting. How could the medium of television be both self-evidently inferior and yet offer such a potent threat to its vastly superior relative? How was it that the entertainment it offered could be both self-evidently moronic and yet so slyly corrosive of American values?

The paradox hardly mattered. From the late fifties onwards television was made to bear a burden that had hitherto fallen exclusively on cinema – that of chief cultural influence and thus chief social polluter. A new candidate had arrived for the role of moral whipping-boy and cinema, which had previously filled the role, was understandably happy to help in wielding the whip, never mind the fact that the circularity of such arguments can be strikingly perverse on occasion. (A good case in point would be Oliver Stone's *Natural Born Killers*, a self-righteous attack on the prurience and amorality of the American news media, which eventually spawned its own copycat crimes – as well as a very old-fashioned controversy on the morally sapping nature of moving pictures.)

The truth was that cinema had good reason to fear the arrival of television, so it is understandable that the portrait it should present to its viewers of what they looked like when they were being unfaithful should be so ugly. Is the light that falls on the audience from a cinema image really that much more flattering than the bluish flicker of the cathode ray tube? Unquestionably, if you believe cinema's version, which discriminates between the two types of spectator with quite explicit prejudice. In film after film you can find scenes in which the television viewer is represented as stupefied, slumped and torpid – sometimes so far gone that they can barely grunt in communication, at other times watching with a glazed inattention that betrays their induced passivity. This prejudicial characterization requires a certain amount of willed myopia. In actuality, television audiences are far more mobile and unruly than cinema audiences;

they are free-range viewers by comparison with the battery hens of cinema, ranged in their stalls and staring fixedly forward. But on film it is generally the television audience that is seen as having abdicated its own identity or capacity for action.

The discrimination can even extend to the way in which we behave when the film or television programme is over. At the end of *The Truman Show*, Peter Weir's fantasy about a man whose entire life proves to be a top-rated documentary soap, representatives of the programme's global audience are shown watching its last ever episode, as Truman Burbank decides to leave his safe but synthetic world for the uncertainty on the other side of the wall. The programme has been running for thirty years, but the loyal fans seem unperturbed at the unexpected withdrawal of their drug. The final scene of the film shows two engrossed policeman chewing on junk food and staring directly at the camera. 'What else is on?' asks one. 'Yeah, what else is on,' replies the other. The endless continuum of television – its appalling promiscuity – will not release them from enchantment in the way in which we are about to be released by the rolling credits. We leave the cinema feeling superior to those hapless consumers – not reflected in their stupefied gaze but flattered by it.

It's true that the prevailing realism of American commercial cinema would tend to produce an association between somnolence and television anyway. A television is a piece of domestic equipment, after all, to be watched in circumstances when the niceties need not be observed. Besides, American households often own more than one set and many of them are watched in bedrooms. But this only amplifies the sense of an overlooked invasion at the very heart of the home. In David Cronenberg's *Videodrome* the slogan for the shabby soft-porn cable station Civic TV is 'The one you take to bed with you'. And the sense that the small screen exerts a kind of baleful, even sinister influence over its audience takes such scenes beyond mere corroborating detail in a realistic setting. When a character watches television on film, the activity is always open to suspicion. It is an act that is frequently emblematic of a kind of ignorance, either literally (in the sense that the screen makes them ignore what they should be concentrating on) or more metaphorically. To watch television is, more often than not, to be distracted, and even when the characters with blue light on their faces are manifestly sympathetic – as they are in the Coen brothers' *Fargo*, say – a residue of contempt remains for the source of that flickering illumination. When Marge Gunderson and her husband end their day in bed, the fact that the television is on accentuates their plain, flat normality.*

There are films that are equally disenchanted by cinema, naturally, but they are usually a good deal more respectful towards the audience. A film like *Matinee*, Joe Dante's satire on B-movie science fiction and the extravagant hype of producers such as William Castle, relishes the mediocrity of what appears on the screen within the screen. But it doesn't, by that token, condemn the audience's enthusiasm, which registers as a kind of lost innocence rather than a stupidity. On the other hand, in a film like *Avalon*, Barry Levinson's hymn to his own Baltimore boyhood, the stupidity of what is seen on television screens implicates the viewers. When the characters first see a television set they stare in amazement at the test patterns on its screen. Content is at first quite superfluous; the astonishment that cinema should have been domesticated is enough in itself. And it isn't long before the new medium has inexorably dissolved the old bonds of family. The raucous meals in which three generations sat together to break bread give way to silent grazing on trays in front of the television. A community has been dissolved before your eyes and even the table – that rectangular altar of familial togetherness – has been broken into individual fragments. (Television, when it acknowledges its own existence at all, is naturally much readier to present television

---

Fargo also includes an instance of a more familiar deployment of the small screen. After the two hit-men have had desultory sex with two hookers, all four are shown sitting up in bed and watching *The Tonight Show*; television is for people who can't sustain ordinary human relationships.

viewing as an act of togetherness. The running gag during the credit sequence for *The Simpsons* shows the family coming together for their one truly unifying activity, the one pleasure that erases their incompatibilities of intelligence and ambition – sitting on the couch and watching the box. *The Simpsons*, incidentally, has offered episodes in which a guilty awareness of parental deficit is corrected by making time *to watch television programmes together*. In this imagined universe, television is the fabric of society, not an acid that eats away at its fibres.)

There's a long list of films that tackle the value system of television in a similar way to *Avalon*, questioning not just its effect on the audience but the essential morality of the industry – from Elia Kazan's *A Face in the Crowd*, which questioned the dangerous ease with which the medium could create celebrities, to Sydney Pollack's *The Electric Horseman*, which satirized the trivializing instincts of the mass media. Numerous others could be added to the list (*Network*, *Broadcast News*, *Being There*, Bertrand Tavernier's *Deathwatch*, Fellini's *Ginger e Fred* and, most recently, *Pleasantville*), but here I want to look more closely at four films in which the presence of television has a peculiarly sinister force.

The first is Douglas Sirk's *All That Heaven Allows*, a suburban melodrama in which Jane Wyman becomes involved in an autumn–summer relationship with Rock Hudson's Thoreauesque tree surgeon ('I don't think Ron's read it,' a friend announces with sublime solemnity after Wyman has read out a famous passage from *Walden*, 'he just lives it'). *All That Heaven Allows* was released in 1955 – at a time when Hollywood was still engaged in hot war with the networks – and its rather febrile account of a socially transgressive love includes a special place for the subversive villainy of the small screen. Wyman's grown-up children are dismayed by their mother's new friendship and attempt to persuade her to break the connection. One of their less confrontational strategies is simple distraction: they make her a present of a television set, an object that offers the dual virtue of restoring some of her social cachet (the device is still novel enough for its arrival to be a special event) and also providing a diverting alternative to her unsuitable romance. It is already clear that Wyman is wary of the device. When one of her friends suggests she buys one to fill the empty hours, she reacts with a slightly surprising asperity. 'Why,' she says quickly, 'because it's supposed to be the last refuge for lonely women?' When her children order one anyway as a surprise Christmas present, the salesman who comes to deliver it pitches its virtues with a jaunty indifference to Wyman's reservations. 'All you have to do is turn that dial and you have all the company you want,' he says as the set is carried in, and Sirk ensures that it is placed so that Wyman's features are reflected in the yellow cast of the screen. You see her isolated and enclosed in that small frame, her daughter, who is sitting beside her on the sofa, effectively edited out by a large red bow around the set, which both obscures her face and exactly matches her dress. This is a large part of the horror of television for film – that it breaks the audience up into lonely individuals. The viewer of the film sees clearly what Wyman as yet only dimly intuits: that this small box is a trap that could contain her life with asphyxiating closeness. The film is rather overloaded with conspicuous emblems of enclosure, from a gridded screen by the door to the glazing bars of the windows, through which she frequently stares in wistful melancholy, but this is the most inventive of all Sirk's cages. Inside it Wyman appears jaundiced and melancholy, a monochrome vision quite unlike the saturated colour Sirk's much larger frame allows her.

In *All That Heaven Allows*, television is presented as a possession that might have the power to possess, but it isn't an actively malign object. It represents only the fate to which Wyman might abandon herself: a colourless half life as a spectator, rather than an actor in the world. In *Poltergeist*, by contrast, the television screen is a conduit to a malevolent world. It is through the blizzard of post-transmission noise that the first seductive calls come to the little girl whose family have had the ill-fortune – or bad judgement – to buy a home located over an Indian burial ground. Given the social anxieties of the period in which *Poltergeist* was made – a time when the apparently irresolvable question of whether television was a good or a bad influence kept up a continuous background mutter – there is something darkly witty about the image with which the film begins. A small child sits before a screen that is not depicting violence or sexual acts or amoral cynicism. It depicts absolutely nothing – the regular chaos known as 'snow'.* And when a voice begins to emerge from that informationless fuzz, part of the *frisson* for us is a doubt about whether we have imagined it – or conjured it. The parents sleep on, oblivious to the menace in their own bedroom. In *Poltergeist* the television literally becomes a portal to hell – an unusually concrete realization of the wilder denunciations of the religious right against the demoralizing effect of television. It is a clever twist, but this is not the only film that has interpreted television's ability to absorb its audience with a horrifying literalism. Indeed, we might venture a generalization here, though it amounts to a hunch rather than a proven fact. It is this: in fantasies that involve some kind of passage through the screen, television mostly swallows the world while film spills new elements out into it. In other words, television is perceived as a black hole, sucking objects out of the real world, while film is

*Digital noise or television 'snow' has always had a peculiar enchantment for film-makers, often because it can be used to lull audiences into a vaguely hypnotic daze that is then shattered by the reappearance of an image. But it is also because the image of noisy chaos offers a kind of flattery to the meaningful order of the cinema screen itself. Watching television 'snow' on a cinema screen, we see both a failure of transmission and an achievement of representation – a vast and perfect rendering of a technological breakdown that we know to be alien to the machinery of the cinema. There is a kind of triumph at such moments, but also a fascination with the glittering animation of this particular kind of blank. 'Snow' allows film to remove all images from the screen without having to give up movement, a signal for the cinema viewer that the film still has its own vitality.

a cornucopia that adds new ones to it.* So in films like *The Purple Rose of Cairo* and *The Last Action Hero*, characters in the onscreen movie escape from their projected world to cause mayhem in the real one (or rather the fictional one that just happens to be one representational layer closer to us), while in *Poltergeist* and David Cronenberg's *Videodrome*, the television screen is liable to ingest elements of the real world into an unseen or horrifying otherworld.

This is given particularly graphic form in one of the hallucinatory passages of *Videodrome*, in which a depicted mouth – that of Debbie Harry – threatens to absorb James Woods's entranced viewer. At the Cathode Ray Mission, down and outs can sit in cubicles watching television, an activity that will 'help patch them back into the world's mixing board'. But this charitable instinct is at odds with the film's chief plot. 'A battle for the mind of North America will be fought in the videodrome,' says the media pundit Brian O'Blivion (who himself exists *only* on television, in the form of a library of posthumous tapes). 'Television is reality and reality is less than television,' he adds later. The syllogism may be faulty but the argument is clear nonetheless. What James Woods discovers in the film is that the pathology of television is not simply a metaphor. Members of a fundamentalist group have created a subterranean channel broadcasting murder and torture, a channel that has been designed to attract precisely the right kind of victims, those that the organizers of this scheme wish to eliminate. A

---

*There are, of course, notable exceptions to this generalization. In Buster Keaton's *Sherlock Jr.*, Keaton enters the world of the screen, the only traffic coming in the other direction being the romantic attitudes that colour his behaviour in the real world. And in Joe Dante's contribution to *Twilight Zone: The Movie*, there's a rare example of television spilling out into the world, through the psychic powers of a ten-year-old boy who has learnt everything he knows from television. Neither, though, quite serves to overrule the broad sense that interaction with film is potentially liberating and exciting, while interaction with television is dangerous and to be resisted. Film enriches the world, television impoverishes it – a general rule given particularly vivid realization in Gary Ross's *Pleasantville*, in which the monochrome universe of a television soap is transformed to rich, saturated colour by the arrival of two contemporary teenagers.

subliminal signal carried by the channel 'induces a brain tumour in the viewer' – in other words, it is a eugenic project that depends entirely on unwitting volunteers. Cronenberg's point is presumably to satirize the fundamentalism of the moral majority (at whose hands he has suffered more than once), but his pursuit of dark thrills can't help but put him in their camp. In *Videodrome* the enemies of violent or sexual imagery tell nothing but the truth: television *does* make society sick. Though Cronenberg's own position is one of pure anti-censorship, he has made a film that appears to underwrite it, as if the long cinematic hatred of television has blurred the clarity of his own principles. Besides, if television is a social carcinogen, then what exactly does that make cinema?

Film will always have a difficulty in pointing the finger in this way – identifying a source of social malaise in the shape of a moving image. But that hasn't stopped it regularly vilifying a medium of obviously close kinship. It helps, naturally, if the broadcasting forces to be reviled are relatively new on the scene. In *The Cable Guy*, Ben Stiller's underrated 1996 comedy, the real object of the satire is less the networks – now venerable enough to be protected from such assault – than the massive proliferation of television outlets, an industrial evolution that has degraded the experience of viewing yet further. *The Cable Guy* begins with a favourite image in cinema about television: the coarse, pixellated dots of a magnified screen. But it adds to that conventional visual symbol of degradation (a term, it's worth remembering, that applies equally to image quality and moral value) another register of television's deficiency as a medium: the zapping instability of attention. Televisions are always represented on film as inimical to mental concentration. They jerk rapidly through the channels, mincing communication into an indigestible babble. It matters, too, that there is a conspicuous contrast between the frantic confusion of what we are looking at and the steadiness and fine grain of the film image that shows it to us.

It is important that we sense the unblinking nature of the

camera in observing this pathological symptom, because an implicit comparison is part of the point. Film is almost always at pains to make television look worse than itself – an easy achievement given the comparative technologies of display. (In the late eighties in Britain, when there were real concerns about falling cinema attendances, this representational rivalry was given explicit form in a generic advert for the pleasures of the cinema. If I've remembered it correctly, a full-screen display of the sort of visual splendours you could expect at your local cinema was followed by the image suddenly diminishing – exactly like the dwindling dot of light that appeared when an old-fashioned set was turned off – until it was no more than a tiny rectangle, the same size as the average television screen. At the same time, the cinema sound suffered an equivalent shrivelling, from multi-speaker resonance to the boxy squawk of a tiny speaker. The vast expanse of projected darkness that surrounded that little light was a powerful piece of rhetoric – this is a battle between a giant and a dwarf, it said. The rhetoric was powerful enough, certainly, to suppress the obvious question for a time: why the giant should even be worried about the contest at all.)

The Cable Guy offers an unusually pure (or at least unusually shameless) example of cinema's hypocrisy with regard to the corrupting effects of television. The film itself is a darkly comic version of the stalker plot, with Jim Carrey's cable technician forming a passionate attachment to Matthew Broderick's lonely yuppie, recently parted from his girlfriend and peculiarly susceptible to the blend of naked need and emotional blackmail that Carrey deploys. Carrey's psychosis obviously has its origin in a deprived childhood, when the early staples of network broadcast were used as a substitute for loving care. 'I never met my father,' he confesses to Broderick, while the two men recline in a giant satellite dish reminiscing about the past, 'but the old TV was always there for me.' In a later sequence, a close-up of Broderick's eyes watching the screen fades into those of Carrey, staring with a glazed fixity that in turn fades to a flashback of his eyes as a child. As his mother prepares to go out to a singles bar he stares blankly at his only dependable companion, the sole evidence of parental concern being his mother's parting words: 'Don't sit so close to that thing – or it'll rot your brain.' The growing menace of his obsession is even represented through a set – when Broderick returns to his flat to find that an enormous home entertainment system has been installed in his living room during his absence. The device is a juggernaut of stupidity that threatens to crowd out the life he has made for himself (the scene strikes up some distinct echoes with Sirk's film – a lonely man recoiling from the siren consolations of television).

When, at the film's conclusion, Carrey decides to kill himself, he does so by throwing himself into the satellite dish that feeds out the poisoning signals. 'Don't you understand, Stephen?' he asks Matthew Broderick's character. 'Somebody has to kill the baby-sitter.' His long fall in slow motion is an enormously extended montage of all the broadcasts he is about to interrupt, including countless hypnotized figures watching their screens as they wait for the cliffhanger verdict in a sensational trial. One is of particular interest: the only figure seen alone, a plump, balding man whose expression is vacant and whose eyes are dull. He is a casting director's idea of the ordinary joe, of middling brow and thickening waist. When the screen goes black, he grunts in surprise and then his liberated eyes stray slowly to a book that looms in the foreground. He picks it up and opens it. The soundtrack modulates to a spring-like string phrase as his face breaks into a faint smile. This is, of course, a joke about cinematic conventions for the lifting of the curse – all those occasions in films when the world magically resumes its sweet normality. But it is also perfectly consonant with cinema's myth of television: that it is a numbing form of mind control, utterly depraving in its intellectual effects.* It may

*The only time that watching television is shown in the film without an undertone of disapproval is when Broderick attempts to reconcile himself with his ex-girlfriend by inviting her round for a meal, a glass of wine, and a night in front of the box – but crucially what they watch is a movie, *Sleepless in Seattle*. In other words, television is only acceptable when it acts as a conduit for the unifying virtues of cinema.

dawn on you at this point that Hollywood itself was never conspicuous for its encouragement of literacy. However much it tried to assume the dignity of literature – whether by hiring prize-winning writers to work on scripts or introducing films with credit sequences of turning pages – the last thing it wanted the audience to do was stay at home and read a good book.

But it hardly needs saying that the cinema audience is never depicted with the same hostility or sense of admonition as television watchers. Film audiences, by contrast, usually sit alert and focused. Their gaze is represented, more often than not, as a sanctified kind of rapture – not the moronic gape of the television slave but a reverent, responsive attention. And where they are inattentive – as they are in several films – it is because the society of the cinema is expressing itself, that twilit communal space that encloses and permits human life rather than extinguishing it.

Going to the cinema is always a participation in society rather than a withdrawal from it, a place for courtship and community.* In a film such as Giuseppe Tornatore's *Cinema Paradiso*, a lament for the dissipation of society under the influence of television that is just as lachrymose as *Avalon*, it can easily feel as though it were the communality of cinema-going that was its defining merit, rather than the accumulated virtues of the films themselves – which are merely the occasion for a raucous congregation. In one of *Cinema Paradiso*'s more elaborate moments of transcendence, Philippe Noiret, the old projectionist, splits the beam of the projector with a pane of glass, reflecting a second image back out of the building and on to a wall in the town square, in front of which a large crowd exclaim their pleasure, moved by the film just as a wheat field

*This is true even when the participation in society might be thought of as disreputable – as in Barry Levinson's *Diner*, a film that includes a scene in which one of the characters wins a bet that he can get his straight-laced girlfriend to touch his penis, by pushing it through the bottom of a box of popcorn they are sharing. Even the scene in *Gremlins*, in which the mischievous demons riot as they watch *Snow White and the Seven Dwarfs*, offers a sense of cinema-going as a carnival of shared pleasure.

is moved by the wind. There is a danger in such rapture: the projectionist's fascination with the magic he has wrought makes him neglect the projector, and when the volatile stock jams the result is a fire that blinds him and burns the theatre to the ground.

But such Promethean punishment has an entirely different tenor to it than the Grand Guignol savagery of a film like *Halloween* – in which the teenagers engrossed in a special holiday screening of *The Thing* remain fatally unconscious of the danger behind them. To watch films in *Cinema Paradiso* is to be hungry for a world outside the village, even if that appetite is continually thwarted by the priest's insistence on censoring every carnal act, so that the kissing scenes that the villagers watch consist of a brutal splicing of anticipation and dreamy aftermath. By contrast, to watch television in *Halloween* is to be fatally myopic about the dangers that immediately surround you. One is a sin of knowledge, the other of ignorance.

If cinema had not picked at this wound so steadily, it would have long since healed. But ill-suppressed animosity alone cannot account for the way in which televisions feature so regularly onscreen, and the truth is that the device had very powerful attractions to offset its offence of usurpation, attractions that made it impossible for directors simply to ignore cinema's stunted rival. There are perfectly straightforward reasons why televisions are so ubiquitous in films: as an essentially realist medium, cinema wishes to depict the world around it, and televisions are increasingly ubiquitous objects in that world. But the privileged presence of televisions within the setting of so many movies is further guaranteed by the device's exceptional utility as an expressive object.

Over the same period, for example, telephones have similarly penetrated public and private spaces, but although film has fully exploited the telephone as a prop in its narratives, the appearance of a telephone is rarely as fraught with potential as the appearance of a television. It opens up for cinema a whole new seam of effects. Some of these are very simple – directors have always been alert to the utility of reflective objects and the television added a new one to the familiar repertoire of mirrors and windows and anything with a sufficiently reflective sheen. Sirk quickly found a use for a low-level mirror and so did Hitchcock, always a greedy exploiter of props; in *North by Northwest* it is the betraying reflection of the television screen that gives away Cary Grant's hiding place when he is being held against his will.

But a television, as a machine that talks without listening, also offers a potent emblem for certain failures of human communication. In *Raging Bull*, Scorsese uses a malfunctioning television as a kind of lightning rod in the scene in which De Niro has a vicious, disconnected argument with his brother. He pounds the set with rage, finding in it a fit (and convenient) scapegoat for his own failures of reception and transmission. After he has attacked his brother and his wife he stares at it, his own blankness reflected in its blankness – as if seeing an image of unmendable defectiveness. And while other objects would have performed these functions, they would not have done it so well. A mirrored cocktail cabinet might have met Hitchcock's functional requirement of exposing Grant's attempt at evasion, but it would not have offered him the satisfying visual pun of a switched-off set giving out a 'picture'. Similarly, an old valve radio might have served equally well for Scorsese, but it could not have supplied that flickering, erratic abstraction of De Niro's inarticulate rage.

Television is also matchless as a new way for injecting information into certain types of drama. Its own narrative instincts, to 'update stories' and bring you 'new developments', have meant that it is an indispensable component of many disaster movies, where it is used to move the action forward economically or to bind disparate characters together by means of shared information. This communicative ability is sometimes even implicated within the plot-line of the film, as it was in the second of the *Die Hard* movies, where the conscienceless opportunism of a television news reporter plays a dangerous role in pushing the action forward. In other films the television news presenter functions as a kind of choral figure, clarifying circumstances and context from within a frame where such activities are entirely natural. Just how well it can perform this role was demonstrated by Baz Luhrmann in his strenuously cool version of *Romeo and Juliet*, a film in which the Prologue is delivered by one of those big-hair, big-smile newsreaders so popular on American television. Shakespeare's explicatory opening lines absorbed the practised gravity and urgent cadences of the 'breaking story' with astonishing ease.

But there is far more substantial temptation that television represents for a director and we can find a clue to what it is in one of the films we've just been considering. During the flash-back sequence in *The Cable Guy* you are briefly shown what the young boy is watching. As his mother leaves he reaches for the dial (this is well before the days of television's real capacity for paralysis, when the only movement needed to change the perceived world is the tap of a finger) and switches to a channel showing *Play Misty for Me*. As you see it, the clip is not self-explanatory – that is, if you haven't seen Eastwood's thriller about a one-night stand that leads to psychotic dependency and murder, this brief extract will not give you enough information to understand the allusion. For those who do recognize it, however, the quotation is quite explicit in its purpose: it hints that what we have taken for an uneasy comedy may yet take a horrific turn.

What's more, television permits this specifically literary device of quotation to fit seamlessly into the imagined world of the film. *Play Misty for Me* is present both as a consistent narrative detail (the first seed of Carrey's own psychosis) and as a dark and useful joke on the part of the director. It is – in a way that a literary quotation would find more difficult to achieve as casually – both an incidental detail and a fairly significant element of the film's emotional colouring.

It's also worth noting here that the cinematic literacy of a whole generation of American directors was the result of their education at the hands of television, which delivered to them the back-catalogue of Hollywood, at that time not easy to find elsewhere. To be 'well viewed' (as people are well read) used to be far more difficult than it is now – in an era of video recordings and cable movie channels. In that respect, television – the ostensible enemy of film culture – actually helped to consolidate and preserve it.*

Similarly, Carpenter's use of *The Thing* in *Halloween* is not simply arbitrary; it pays homage to a classic horror film, yes, and it plays cleverly with the distinction between two kinds of imagined terror – the antique one that holds few fears for us and the contemporary one that currently has us in its grasp.† But in addition to providing an ironic interaction between an immediate threat and a displaced one, that brief appearance by *The Thing* carries another faint current: a reminder that the most despised of genres, horror, has its canonical works and that we might conceivably be watching another one now.

This kind of allusion reaches its apotheosis in Wes Craven's *Scream*, in which the teenage victims are all experts in the mechanics of the genre in which they find themselves and in which a paused video of *Halloween* provides an allusive backdrop to one of the murders. *Scream* also brilliantly exploits the television as a device for layering together different kinds of

---

*Video has also introduced the general public to an experience that used to be reserved only for technicians: that of spooling through film, reversing it, subjecting it to our commands. Watching a film in a cinema, we always know our place, because it is always *now*, the moment selected by the director. When we watch a film on video, insurrection is always there at the press of a button.
†Is there any more perishable substance than cinematic terror? *Nosferatu* remains a wonderful film, the pioneer of many ways of stirring dread in an audience. It even contains an early model for one of Carpenter's most celebrated effects in *Halloween* – the sequence in which a ghost-white face slowly appears out of blackness, which is prefigured by Murnau's sequence in which the vampire advances on its victim from the darkness of an adjoining room. But *Nosferatu* is not frightening today in the way that a Keaton comedy remains funny. We laugh without irony or scholarship, but to be genuinely terrified by *Nosferatu* requires an act of historical reconstruction. What must it have been like to watch this, then?

inattention – one of the climactic scenes involves the heroine watching a boy on a television screen watching a television screen on which the characters are watching a television screen. As he utters warnings to the oblivious characters in *Halloween*, the killer is silently approaching behind him and he himself is the subject of appalled cries of warning from his powerless observers, looking at the scene from a television feed in a news crew's broadcast van. It is hard to imagine that this cat's-cradle of helpless surveillance could be exceeded in terms of complexity.

Quotation in any art form is rarely a simple act of homage; it acknowledges a predecessor partly in order to stake a claim of equivalence, and this is just as true of film as it is of literature. The process may be more complex in cinema, because the representational deficiency of a classical quotation is always likely to render it vulnerable to affectionate condescension. The fuzziness of the monochrome picture and the boxiness of the sound establish it in a position of technological subservience to the film in which it appears. But the unsettling blend of respect and competition is there nonetheless, and it is emphasized by the possibility, always present, that we might prefer to watch the quoted film rather than the one that enfolds it. We know that the film within the film has a real existence independent of this set and these actors; it is a real object that brings with it a crowd of associations that predate and exceed the slice of reality in which we are currently agreeing to believe. What's more, it finds itself at a distinct advantage with regard to other objects in the film because – except when seen in a very diminished or distorted form – it is not merely a *representation* of a film but the thing itself. It would be quite possible, were the clip long enough, to become engrossed in that film instead, to 'take it for real', something that is doubly true when the quotation fills the frame. No amount of concentration will do the same for any other real object onscreen. We cannot drive the car we see or taste the coffee that looms in the foreground, but we can consume the film within the film. It will be flavoured by what it is immersed in, naturally, but the process of consumption is to all intents and purposes precisely as it would have been in a conventional screening.

Cinema Paradiso also demonstrates the ability of such incorporated projections to make us forget the imagined world of the film we are watching. In the scene already described, where the film is projected into the village square, the image is projected on to the façade of a villager's house. At one point he emerges on his balcony to find himself a ghostly presence in an Italian romantic comedy. But after he is catcalled and jeered at by the audience below, he withdraws and closes his shutters again, and the vivid particulars of this impromptu screen effectively disappear as the vintage film begins to work upon us. We look through it to the illusory space of the cinema world, a black-and-white universe that makes us forget what lies behind that façade, just as Tornatore's film has made us forget what lies behind the screen in front of us.

Of course, quotation and allusion in the cinema did not have to wait for the arrival of television; it is possible to think of numerous scenes in which the book a character is reading will give us a clue, either as to the psychological components of their behaviour or to possible developments in the plot. Douglas Sirk, as we've seen, deploys Thoreau's *Walden* with just such billboard subtlety – a classic instance of a melodrama clutching at substantiality. (Indeed, *All That Heaven Allows* might be said to be poised rather precisely between an old practice and a new. Sirk does not exploit the possibilities of what can be presented on that television screen; it is still to books that he turns for allusive interplay.) Nor is the self-referential touch the preserve of modern cinema. F.W. Murnau's *Faust* begins with a puppeteer performing a devilish shadow play on a large sheet – a kind of ur-cinema that serves almost as a claim of pedigree by the new rt form. Allusion had clearly been available, too, from the first moment when signatures of style began to impress themselves upon the celluloid. But the arrival of television makes it a great deal easier for film to quote itself without a breach of the prevailing naturalistic etiquette – not for the first time exactly (there had been films about films well before the arrival of television), but certainly with a casualness and intimacy that is never quite achievable if you need another cinema screen to do it.*

When, in *Mean Streets*, for example, Scorsese wishes to 'quote' John Ford's *The Searchers*, he arranges a trip to the cinema to do it. This is to the point, of course – *Mean Streets* is infused and informed by Scorsese's own adolescence, in which the cinema was central. What's more, American urban life without the movies is virtually unthinkable. The fact that this scene slightly disrupts our expectations tells you as much about the conventional reticence of cinema in referring to itself (just as television soaps about ordinary families almost never show them doing that most ordinary thing: watching a soap) as it does about the significance of the particular film shown. But the fact that *The Searchers* is so conspicuously out of period remains a moment of strain in the film's otherwise easy depiction of this world and its manners.

Mean Streets is a self-conscious film, conspicuously aware of the moves it makes, but even so this moment stands slightly proud of the film's surface. While you can just about imagine that Harvey Keitel might have a passion for the classics of American cinema, it's more difficult to believe that his friends would have gone along with the suggestion quite so affably. Scorsese wants to quote the wedding party fight scene from *The Searchers*, a Western prototype for the almost amiable violence that periodically breaks out in his own film (and that proves such a lulling prelude to his shocking ending). But even as you absorb the reference, you can't help wondering what these characters might have gone to see if the excursion had been about their own entertainment rather than the director's sense of Hollywood history. If the narrative is taken to be roughly

*A simpler way of putting this would be to say that film quotation suddenly becomes available to films that are not ostensibly about film-making.

contemporaneous with its release (1973), they would have had a wide choice: *The Godfather* would probably still have been running in New York (it opened the previous year), but they might equally have gone to see *Magnum Force*, *American Graffiti*, *High Plains Drifter*, John Milius's *Dillinger* or *Day of the Jackal*, each one of which would have supplied its own distinctive confrontation between cinematic myth and the private movies we run in our own heads. (It offers an intriguing thought experiment to consider alternative possibilities, too. What would this scene have looked like if they had decided to watch *Everything You Always Wanted to Know About Sex but Were Afraid to Ask*? It seems unthinkable, but why exactly? Is it because a comedy might arouse in us – the true audience – the wrong kind of interest? Or is it because the surrender of your own audience to another director's work is a moment fraught with anxieties – anxieties that may be subdued if the rival is dead or safely fixed in the canon.)

In *The King of Comedy*, by contrast, Scorsese uses a television set for quotation, showing a brief clip from Bresson's *Pickpocket* on a television screen in Jerry Lewis's apartment. The moment is quite different in its effect – an almost fugitive reference that does not push itself forward (in the way the passage from *The Searchers* literally does, at one point effectively erasing the film in which it appears, when it is shown full screen). With television, films can appear in passing and they can appear not in the unique and specialized venues designed for the projection of films but in a domestic interior (and exterior, too, if the set happens to be in a shop front). A new device becomes available: the ironic interference between an image made in very different circumstances and the events that unfold in its light.

The exploitation of this potential is for the most part coarse. One thinks of the familiar sequence in which a confrontation is arranged between a scene of atrocity and the simulated vivacity that continues to pour out of the screen. In a silent room a family lies murdered but the television continues to pour out its inane simulation of direct contact. Such scenes convey a strange notion of the consciencelessness of television, its duplicity in appearing to care for the audience when it can't possibly, because it is actually blind to their circumstances. The accusation is preposterously unfair – as though any piece of machinery might take account of what happens in front of it – but it delivers a dependable *frisson* nonetheless, dependable enough to make this a stock effect in movies.

There are other variations on this theme of the dissonance between broadcast and reception. In Joseph Ruben's *The Stepfather*, the protagonist, a psychopathic perfectionist who has been marrying into fatherless families and then slaughtering them wholesale when they disappoint him, is shown at one point chuckling at an old episode of *Mr Ed*. It is as if this taste alone will confirm his dangerous detachment from reality – he wants a television family, not the real kind.

Curiously enough, on one of the few occasions I can think of in which a killing is shown to take place in front of a cinema screen, the film image *does* appear to respond to what is taking place in front of it. In Hitchcock's *Saboteur*, one of the fugitives is distracted by the scene being projected in the cinema in which he has taken refuge. The dialogue just happens to match his circumstances exactly. He turns to see a giant revolver onscreen, the actor apparently addressing him directly. He is then shot through the screen in perfect synchronization with the recorded percussion of the projected weapon. But I don't think one could derive any generalization from this scene, except for a sense of Hitchcock's voracious opportunism when it came to visual games.

Far more crucially, television offers film another way to incorporate documents within itself. And it is here – in the incorporation of accidental and home-made forms of television (in particular security cameras and home video) – that cinema finds itself forced to arrive at a new modus vivendi with the usurping medium. The grain of a television image comes to represent not an impoverishment of representation but an enrichment of veracity. These codes frequently overlap; it is possible, for example, for pixellation both to confirm the corruption of an image (if what you see is a television evangelist, say) and its purity (if what you see is notionally footage from a surveillance camera), but the latter sense – that this is an unadulterated kind of vision – increases in strength as time passes.

Again this effect is hardly an invention of television. Martin Scorsese has described the way in which his generation of students at New York Film School responded to the impact of the Zapruder film – the 8mm home-movie camera footage of the assassination of President Kennedy. The Zapruder footage is the shortest sequence to have been selected for preservation by America's National Film Registry and the only home movie so honoured. The Registry selects twenty-five films a year that are deemed 'culturally, historically and aesthetically important', and while it might first appear that the Zapruder footage qualifies by virtue of the second category, it wouldn't be difficult to make out a fairly good case for its significance as an artistic influence. For Scorsese and his circle, the phrase 'the Zapruder factor' came to serve as shorthand for a sense of immediacy and drama that was directly related to the deficiencies of the footage in cinematic terms. Zapruder's framing was shaky, his focus off, his stock cheap and grainy, but the impact of this short roll of film had a real effect on film-makers.

It can't have done any harm that Zapruder's contingent masterpiece coincided with a whole series of other experiments in which perfection of finish was sacrificed for intensity of content. From the Nouvelle Vague in France to the British Free Cinema movement, film-makers everywhere were responding to the new possibilities of portable sync-sound equipment (and when the equipment didn't yet exist jury-rigged versions were created). Well before Kennedy's death, documentarists like Donn Pennebaker and Albert and David Maysles had explored the potential of the new equipment (often in films about Kennedy himself). At the same time, *cinéma vérité* had instituted a new set of criteria by which an image might be judged, a replacement of the Hollywood studio tradition – in which a world was fashioned from scratch – by a kind of inspirational kleptomania, in which the available world could be pillaged for useful goods.

The interaction of all these influences and possibilities is complex, but television was at the heart of them, providing a medium in which new ways of filming could be explored, as well as subsequently providing a point of entry for those techniques into more conventional fiction films. It is worth remembering just how novel these techniques were in the sixties, particularly because the unceasing improvement of lightweight cameras has made the identifying marks of this particular language into an accent of amateurism rather than professional achievement.

Richard Leacock, one of the founding fathers of Direct Cinema, recalled the haphazard production of *Primary*, an observational documentary about John Kennedy's electoral battle with Hubert Humphrey in which the poverty of the equipment induced the birth of a new aesthetic:

> We made a film that captured the flavour, the gust of what was happening. No interviews. No re-enactments. No staged scenes and very little narration. When we returned to New York we showed our film to visiting British documentary film-maker Paul Rotha, he was astounded and said, 'My God! We've been trying to do this for the last forty years and you've done it . . .' He was in tears.

As documentary found itself abandoning the tools of fiction – scripted dialogue and careful set-ups – in pursuit of a more vivid impression of reality, it was perhaps not entirely surprising that some fiction film-makers wished to follow suit. The gap between documentary and feature film had just widened and it could be narrowed again by borrowing the same techniques.

At first these distinctive idioms were more easily achieved on film than by any other means. When Martin Scorsese began *Mean Streets* with a sequence of roughly cut Super-8 cine film, it offered the audience something like an italicized epigraph for the film that was to follow – a distinctive ratio and style that carried with it powerful implications about the nature of what we were viewing. The unconscious syllogism runs something like this: Hollywood film-makers do not generally use cine film stock; cine film is used for the private commemoration of essentially private moments. Therefore, this scene is not really part of a feature film; it is an eruption of found material into a constructed narrative. The sequence is 'documentary' not just in its appropriation of a distinct stylistic language, but because it offers papers of identity to the viewer – who may be wondering whether to allow these characters across the border between the unconvincing and the plausible.

The paradoxical sense that we are encountering the protagonists of the film 'off camera' in such scenes is amplified by self-conscious behaviour that is peculiar to home movies. Harvey Keitel poses and points directly at the lens, engaged in a steady pantomime intercourse with the camera that is the absolute antithesis of the studied unawareness that the film actor must learn. In a conventional feature film the characters may look anywhere but directly at the lens (when they do, in direct address or mannered apostrophes, we are expected to feel the discomfiting sense of a rule being broken). In a home movie they are not really expected to look anywhere else, because the cine camera is an actor in the scene, too, a recording presence that demands some kind of acknowledgement, some demonstrative gesture of pleasure or acquiescence. And curiously, that direct address implies our invisibility – the actor isn't worried about breaking the rules because there is no prospect of an audience for these scenes, other than friends and family who will expect some direct communication.

Unlike feature films, home movies involve no anticipation of public display, and the play between these two incompatible screen languages – the performance that resolutely pretends it isn't and the reality that asserts itself through awkward performance – generates a spark of presence. Which is more real? The defective representation of Super-8, with its transparently acted gestures of conviviality, or the painstaking simulation of life provided by the film that incorporates it? The question seems easily resolved: it must be the cine film surely, in part precisely because it is indifferent to our requirements as paying customers. This is true not just in the ostentatious poverty of the image, but because in most cases its content is not a load-bearing element of the film's narrative architecture. Such interpolations rarely advance a narrative in any substantive way; instead they corroborate or complicate our sense of what the characters are – they provide 'back story', in the jargon of screenwriting. And that freedom from the need to 'stick to a story' gives such moments a powerful aura of authenticity, of honest indifference to the film's commercial purposes.

At the same time, such sequences are at a disadvantage when it comes to engrossing us. We are less likely to lose ourselves in an image that we believe, at some level, to be a fragment of superfluous life, one that overflows the narrative bounds of the film. Moreover, when we watch such sequences onscreen we are unusually aware that they are a mere play of light on a blank surface. They have the poignant two-dimensionality of recalled time, conspicuously detached from the occasions that they record by their graininess and fugitive colours.* Nor can these sequences rely on narrative logic to distract us from their jerky insufficiency in representing real life. They have a fragility, a liability for damage that insists on the fact that they are just celluloid impressions, irretrievably separated from their originals.† The film in which these passages are incorporated, on

---

*It is not very surprising that they are now cinema's best available shorthand for recollection – more vivacious than photography, but possessed of the same qualities of poignant intangibility.
†The physical reality of film is much more conspicuous in a film-within-a-film than it is with the film itself – the edits are suddenly jarring on the eye, an obvious discontinuity that appears distractingly salient. This is because our attention rests on the surface of the film rather then penetrating through it to the imagined world it displays. So the content of the picture has no power to make you forget its means. A similar effect can sometimes be seen when you watch

the other hand, works to deny that gap altogether, to make the audience forget that there is a void between the recording and what was recorded. In its comparative density of colour, steadiness and richness of detail, the film hopes to assert a larger grasp of reality.

The invention of video clearly extends the possibilities of such interactions – partly because it is even more ubiquitous as a form of self-recording than cine film, partly because it greatly diminishes the technical delay between filming and viewing. Video needs no development and that fact means that its suggestion of elapsed time has diminished considerably. Indeed, the act of recording can even be shown as simultaneous with the act of viewing, as it is in Bernardo Bertolucci's *Stealing Beauty*, a film that offers a rather striking example of the video's useful property of allowing the director to disavow authority of a particular image or sequence (the same implicit disavowal that underpins such sequences' claim to authenticity). At the beginning of his tale of a girl's coming of age in Tuscany, Bertolucci offers you images taken with a camcorder on a transatlantic flight. The girl in question is asleep and thus vulnerable to an inspection that she could otherwise deflect with her own stare. The camera nudges and pokes, zooming in close on the crotch of her jeans in a way that feels almost tangibly improper – it is a visual molestation. The image has the coarse texture and smeared contrasts of video, a quality that effectively displaces the offence from Bertolucci to the unknown amateur wielding the camera. It's relatively easy to imagine an identical scene without that insulating screen of pixels – presented as a simple point-of-view shot, for example. But the identity between the film's vision – as expressed in all its other scenes – and that of the unknown voyeur would make the sequence far more

---

the light cast by a television in a house you are passing in the street. What you see is a staccato flicker that seems far too erratic ever to convey a coherent narrative. But when you are watching the screen yourself that spasmodic fluctuation effectively becomes invisible, veiled by an elaborately constructed continuity.

discomfiting, less easily discounted as another person's action (this is clearly a deed, not just an accident in which the gaze has fallen on those particular quarters).

It's possible that this passage is in the nature of a confession from Bertolucci, a reminder that our perceptions of beauty almost always have a predatory appetite to them, whether the object of appreciation is a rural landscape or a human body. It doesn't exactly feel like that, but more like a way of making it absolutely clear that his own form of scrutiny sits above the merely lubricious. His film ends with scene of defloration which, if anything, exceeds the voyeuristic impudence of the opening. As the girl finally surrenders her virginity the camera accompanies her lover's hand on its erotic foray beneath her skirt. You have the feeling that the lens is groping like a truffle pig for the arousing object of its desires. Only the saturation of the colour and the fineness of the grain distinguish it from the gormandizing stare shown at the beginning, but they are sufficient at least to make a case for exoneration.

This sense of a deferred responsibility for the images shown on newsreels or camcorders is also conspicuous when the devices are used to show scenes of extreme violence. Perhaps the classic instance in this case is Michael Powell's *Peeping Tom*, in which a deranged cameraman films the murders that he commits with a sharpened tripod spike. But video perfects the device. It is a recording medium that is effectively insulated from all forms of outside inspection (you don't have to send the tape away for development, after all) and so it is perfectly placed to represent scenes that are either furtive or private. That alone would not account for the affective impact of the device. It delivers at least two other things besides: a jarring discontinuity in visual quality that is likely to resuscitate the viewer's attention; and the implication that this image stands in a relationship of increased realism to the scenes that surround it.

Video also delivers a paradoxical liberty to the director: it allows the indecorous or repulsive to take place effectively 'offscreen' – just as classic Hollywood films would turn aside for a moment of violence – and yet it provides a means for everything to be depicted. In *Henry, Portrait of a Serial Killer*, the videoed murders, watched with retrospective relish by the killer as he relaxes later, reveal to us the appalling savagery of his acts. Will Self has rightly said of these scenes that they are made 'not to be watched'. They take the measure of what we can unblinkingly face. But their degradation in mere technical terms also makes it easier for us to pretend that these are not part of the film we have helped to procure with our ticket money. It is clear that these scenes, with their roller-coaster exposures and wonky angles, are not consistent with the standards we expect from a commercial film. At the same time, you would have to be deranged to go to the manager and ask for your money back on the grounds that they were technically unsatisfactory. They have conspicuously not been made to be viewed by a larger audience. So we have some vestigial sense of privilege in being permitted to see them. (The sense of privilege can persist even if the footage notionally is intended for public display. In *The Blair Witch Project*, the handheld footage delivers an extra charge because of the suggestion that it is all that remains – the fragments are 'raw' technically and emotionally).

This pretence that the recording camera doesn't belong to the director is easy enough to see through – few films have ever been so subservient to the world that their makers can effectively disavow what they contain. But we may be inclined to accept the shaky terms on which the exculpation is offered, simply because we share in its protection. The film doesn't rely on our moral sense to distinguish what should be watched and what shouldn't; it codes that quality into the images themselves, and by doing so it exonerates us, to a degree, from our responsibility to decide. Watching such scenes, we are not, quite so nakedly at least, watching them ourselves. We are watching someone else watching them, and this may implicate us less deeply in the moral question of what it is to be a spectator. Pornography, too, often finds a place on the cinema screen in a diminished frame, not only because this provides a way to mask what would be legally unscreenable, but because in this way we are never in danger of thinking of ourselves as consumers of pornography. To place an image in recession within the screen is always to diminish its power to disgust or arouse. And this is true even when the end result of such recessions is memorably disgusting. The murder scenes in *Henry, Portrait of a Serial Killer* gain in intensity from their presentation as brutal documentary, but may also be legitimized by the same device.

We began with tremor of revulsion and we have arrived now at a kind of tranquillizing recruitment – television not as a demonized harbinger of extinction but as an expressive device fully incorporated into cinema, absorbed by it and made obedient to its own ambitions. Many of those original strains of disgust remain. It appears to have become almost a habit on the part of movie-makers to repeat the old libels, to exploit that flattering comparison between a promiscuous and cheap medium and one that conducts its affairs with more discretion and fine discernment.

Cinema should be more grateful. If only through the power of such contrasts the arrival of television would have consolidated the claims of cinema to be an art form, making more conspicuous the formal conditions of its display. But it contributed to the older form's maturity in far more direct ways, too: by extending its powers of allusion, self-quotation and subtlety of depiction.

Paradoxically, given that television was identified from the very start as a singularly dumb medium – corrupting in its simplifications and its glossy mendacity – it also enlarged cinema's ability to represent reality, to tell stories and to give its images moral depth. In this respect the history of cinema's love–hate relationship with its vulgar cousin may offer a reassurance to those who continue to be perturbed by cinema's vulnerability – in particular those who share the nervous apprehension with which the industry is looking at new competitors in computer games and virtual reality, both of which have also been identified as usurping technologies, media that seduce and mesmerize the audience, diverting them from old loyalties.

Those who value cinema should take some heart from this story of anxiety converted into mastery and exploitation. Cinema has passed through such uncertainties before – times when its nerve failed and its prospects seemed dim. And if it did not exactly prevail (who could sensibly say that television has been defeated?), then it did come to a working accommodation with the enemy, proof that almost anything can be accommodated within the screen and turned to its particular purposes.

INDEX